PAGSL

Frogmen:

First Battles

By
William Schofield
and
P. J. Carisella

Library of Congress Cataloging-in-Publication Data
Schofield, William G. (William Greenough), 1909-
Frogmen : First Battles.

Bibliography: p.
Includes index.
1. World War, 1939-1945 — Naval operations — Submarine. 2.
World War, 1939-1945 — Naval operations — Italian. I. Carisella, P.
J.

II. Title.

D784.I8S36 1987 940.54'5945 87-10317
ISBN 0-8283-1998-7

Branden Publishing Company
17 Station Street
Box 843 Brookline Village
Boston, MA 02147-0843

Contents

Foreword

At the peak of World War II, between March 1941 and September 1943, a small band of daredevil Italian Navymen roved the Mediterranean Sea and raised devastating havoc with British and American shipping.

These were the "frogmen", the pilots of human-torpedoes and self-exploding E-boats. They were the first of their breed, a new type of warrior in the annals of naval conflict. They specialized in swift night-time raids against enemy harbors, operating independently with such dash and abandon that they sometimes deliberately blew themselves to pieces.

In their short span of action, they sank or otherwise knocked out of commission more than 30 ships of the enemy. Their shattered victims ranged from Royal Navy battleships to American cargo carriers, from tankers to destroyers. They spread terror and destruction from Gibraltar to Alexandria, from Algiers to the Crimea. They were the men of the little-known Tenth Light Flotilla, and their commander on their most daring exploits was the legendary "Black Prince of Rome", Commander Valerio Borghese. He had completed his plans and preparations for a surprise attack on New York Harbor, when Italy dropped out of the war.

Winston Churchill, at a secret emergency session of Parliament in 1942, warned the British Government of the crisis being created by these men and described them as possessing "extraordinary courage and ingenuity". He even drew upon Britain's thin line of air defense to despatch planes to the Mediterranean to engage them.

How the raiders of the Tenth achieved their victories in the face of early defeats and incredible odds is the story that is told in these pages.

Nine years of research that went into the preparation of this book dealt for the most part with compiling, cross-checking and confirming the eye-witness accounts of the participants themselves. Thus the story is their own, as related by the Italian Navymen who carried out the extraordinary attacks and the men of the Royal Navy who stood against them.

Bravery and gallantry alike were the elements shared by the principals of both sides in this unique form of naval warfare. The respect that each held for the other was perhaps best exemplified in the relationship that developed between British Admiral Charles Morgan and Italian Lieutenant Luigi Durand de la Penne.

De la Penne, with diver specialist Emilio Bianchi, had attacked and knocked out the British battleship *Valiant* in Alexandria Harbor in December of 1941. Morgan, who was commanding officer of the *Valiant* at that time, later lauded de la Penne for alerting the British that their ship was about to blow up, and Morgan also praised the Italian mariner for valuable services rendered to the Allies following Italy's surrender.

"I did my best to obtain a British decoration for him", said Admiral Morgan in a registered statement made in 1946. "However, as we were officially still at war with the Italian nation, no awards were being granted to Italian Naval Officers.

"In March of 1945," Morgan continued, "Crown Prince Umberto of Italy came down to Taranto, where I was the Admiral Commanding the Adriatic, to inspect the Italian ships and establishments. I lunched with him on the second day and accompanied him during his inspections, which included a visit to St. Vito Barracks where a presentation of medals was to take place.

"The first officer to be decorated with the Italian Gold Medal for Valor — equivalent to our Victoria Cross — was Lieutenant de la Penne for his attack on my ship, *HMS Valiant*, on the night of 18th-19th December, 1941. After the citation had been read out to the parade, Lieutenant de la Penne came forward to the platform. As he did so, the Crown Prince turned round to me and said, 'Come on, Morgan, this is your show!' I stepped forward, took the medal from the Crown Prince's hand, and pinned it on Lieutenant de la Penne's breast. I thus had the pleasure and honor of decorating Lieutenant de la Penne with the highest award granted by the Italian Navy, for the very courageous and gallant attack he had made on my ship three years and three months before!"

De la Penne, incidentally, survived the war and soon thereafter became a member of the Italian Parliament.

Records of the British Admiralty and the Italian Naval Ministry have served to document the saga of the Tenth and in many cases to supply missing dates and incidental details that were necessary to this book.

A special debt of gratitude is owed to the men of both services, Italian and British alike, who so graciously took the time (and no doubt incovenienced themselves) to commit the story of their experiences to letters of correspondence and taped interviews. Many of them eventually received their nation's highest awards for gallantry in action. Many advanced from their days of Mediterranean derring-do to become retired admirals, political leaders or successful industrialists. We thank them all for their generous cooperation in helping to bring this story together. And no summation of gratitude would be complete without acknowledging the many hours of painstaking work contributed by Yolanda Ballou Roberto of Wakefield, Massachusetts, in the areas of translation and transcribing interviews.

Finally, we express special thanks, posthumously, to Prince Valerio Borghese, who wrote an informative chronicle of the achievements of the Tenth Light Flotilla and who died in self-imposed exile in Cadiz, Spain, in August, 1974. The Prince, it seems, had never acknowledged Italy's surrender.

As the leader of his spirited band of frogmen, Borghese once said, "We'll put our heads into the lion's mouth without his knowing it." This they did.

W. S.
P. J. C.

Manned torpedo used by Italy in World War I.

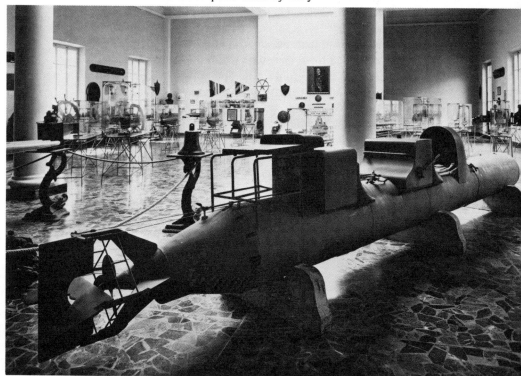

Human-torpedo used by Tenth Light Flotilla frogmen.

Chapter 1.
Target New York

On a warm and humid night in June of 1942, Prince Valerio Borghese of the Italian Royal Navy was a dinner guest at German Submarine Headquarters on the Bois de Boulogne in Paris.

The Prince was a Commander in the submarine arm of his government's Naval Ministry, Supermarina. His host for the evening was also a skilled submariner, but on a much loftier level. He was Admiral Karl Doenitz, Commander-in-Chief of Germany's *untersee* fleet, designer and director of deadly U-boat wolfpack tactics, bane of Anglo-American shipping in the war-ridden North Atlantic.

At that point in World War II, Doenitz had lived through enough victories and disappointments as to be virtually immune to shock or surprise, regardless of origin. But Borghese's words just now had jolted him to attention at the dinner table. He stopped eating and stared at the Italian.

"Repeat that, please."

Borghese nodded and took a sip of his wine. "We intend to attack New York Harbor," he said. "Our plan is to carry the war up the Hudson River and into the heart of the city. We're fully prepared to handle the operation ourselves, but we need your logistical support."

"So you'll attack New York." The Admiral continued to stare at him. "With what?"

"With our Tenth Light Flotilla," Borghese replied. "With our explosive motorboats, and our two-man submarine teams and our human torpedoes — using them exactly as we used them to sink the British battleships at Alexandria. The same way we sank the *Denby Dale* at Gibraltar. And the way our E-boats sank four ships in one night at Suda Bay.

"And at Malta last July?" Doenitz mocked. "When your Tenth Light was almost wiped out?"

Borghese winced. "The attack on Malta was a mistake from the beginning. I was not in command of the Tenth at that time. My appointment came later, after the slaughter. Several of us risked our careers to argue against the Malta operation. It was an impossible mission. We recognized from the start that it could mean only one thing — inevitable, glorious suicide, which is a gross contradiction in terms because suicide is never inevitable — "

"And there is no glory in giving one's life for a meaningless gesture," Doenitz broke in. He lit up a thin cigar and waved aside the rising smoke. "Why do you think New York would be more successful?"

"Because of our record since the debacle at Malta," Borghese replied. "Malta was a turning point. All of our attacks since then have been successful."

"Man learns from his mistakes," Doenitz agreed. "Especially in time of war. Otherwise he goes into the history books as just another integral statistic, and none of us enjoys that dismal prospect."

Abruptly the Admiral changed the subject. "Tell me, Commander," he said, leaning back from the table. "What has impressed you the most about this dinner we're enjoying?"

"An easy question," Borghese smiled. "What impresses me the most is the fact that here at Submarine Headquarters we're eating as peasants might eat. That tells me something."

"So?"

"Yes. Since you Germans occupied Paris, the assumption in the world outside has been that you're enjoying orgiastic feasts, drinking the finest of wines, gorging on tender steaks and the tongues of peacocks, reveling with beautiful women in soft beds, as becomes a conquering power."

"All of which I could bring about with a snap of my fingers," Doenitz remarked. "The black market operations here in Paris are unprecedented in military history. The opportunities are tempting. We could be dining on the choicest of delicacies and washing our women's feet in champagne, if we wished."

"Yes."

"And some of my countrymen are doing exactly that," Doenitz went on. "The officers of the SS and the Luftwaffe, for example." He paused for emphasis. "But that is not the way of the submariner," he continued. "We are a hard lot, strongly disciplined. We believe in obeying wartime restrictions to the letter. And so when you dine as my guest, Prince Borghese, what do you get? For luncheon, a bowl of weak cabbage soup, two centimeters of cheese squeezed out of a tube, two slices of black bread, and a single glass of wine. And perhaps at dinner, a piece of veal or rabbit. Do you understand why I am making a point of all this, Commander?"

Borghese's nod was brief. "I believe I do."

Doenitz studied him in silence for a moment. He was familiar with the younger officer's background and bloodline. He knew Borghese to be authentic Roman royalty, descendant of an ancient Tuscan family that had known power and pomp for more than 400 years, a family line that included the 17th century Pope Paul V, a lineage of soldiery and savantry, of ruthlessness and bravery, intrigue and loyalty. Borghese, at 35, was the romantic woman's concept of how an Italian nobleman should look and conduct himself. In Rome, they called him the "Black Prince."

"Yes," Doenitz observed at last. "You do — you understand. You are a born Fascist, Commander, and I do not always approve of that political philosophy. But you are also a man of perception and intellect, one who recognizes that the ability to control men rests in the ability to control one's self. There cannot be one without the other. And your record shows your awareness of that truth."

"Thank you, Admiral."

"I am familiar, Prince Borghese, with the history of the Tenth Light Flotilla," the Admiral continued. "They have aroused my sympathy and my esteem. They have fought against incredible odds and they have won incredible victories. You come to me with good credentials."

Borghese nodded, letting his thoughts trail back across the past fifteen months. Besides a heavy cruiser, *HMS York*, three merchant cargo ships totaling 32,000 tons had been sunk in the attack on Suda Bay. The following September at Gibraltar, when the huge naval tanker *Denby Dale* had gone down, torpedoes of the Tenth Light had also sunk the armed motorship *Durham* and the tanker *Fiona Shell*. And in the brilliant December attack on Alexandria, six of the Tenth Light torpedomen had knocked out a 10,000-ton tanker plus the Royal Navy's last two Mediterranean-based battleships, the *Queen Elizabeth* and the *Valiant* of 32,000 tons each.

"But," Doenitz was saying, "it takes more than good credentials to guarantee a successful attack against New York. It will take, at the least, many months of careful planning and preparation, a superlative effort on the part of all concerned, and a prodigious amount of good luck. Tell me — what do you ask of me in the way of assistance?"

Borghese relaxed. For the first time since his meeting with Doenitz, he felt that the German leader would be willing to cooperate. Admiral Bertoldi, representing the Italian Navy in Berlin, had been unable to spark the German High Command into committing itself one way or another on the proposal to strike at New York. But here in Paris, it appeared that Doenitz was willing at least to listen to the particulars of the mission, and perhaps to engage himself personally in helping to launch it. If so, there would be no prohibitive reason not to attempt it.

"Naturally there can be no guarantee of success." Borghese said. "You are right, it requires more than credentials. But we are not only willing to try, we are eager. And we have shown that we know what to do and how to do it."

Doenitz nodded agreement.

"What I am asking," Borghese went on, "Is permission to go through your files for information reports concerning strategic harbors of North America, Brazil and South Africa. Yes, those others too, for if we're successful against New York we shall plan similar attacks against Freetown and elsewhere.

"But New York is our primary target. I should like to study reports on traffic volume through the harbor, the regular stations for warships, the convoy assembly areas, the defense systems, the hydrographic characteristics, and any such data that may be available.

"We propose to take one of our ocean-going submarines — preferably the *Leonardo Da Vinci*, now at Bordeaux — and rebuild her deck to equip her for carrying two of our midget submarines, each armed with two torpedoes.

"The *Da Vinci* would transport the submarines and other assault units to the mouth of New York Harbor. There they would be detached and sent off to get past the harbor nets. Our men are experts at that. They would have no problem getting into the Hudson River and launching their attack."

"And then?"

"And then!" Borghese's eyes brightened with excitement. "Psychologically, it would be a staggering blow against the United States. Militarily, it would force them to pull back some of their high-seas units to positions of coastal defense. They would not know where or when the next attack might be expected. Boston, perhaps? Or Norfolk? And the result? — more freedom of action and better fighting conditions for you, in your war against the convoy lanes. Widespread fear and panic in the United States. And a tremendous lift for all men who are fighting for the Axis cause."

Doenitz studied the ash at the end of his cigar. Then, looking up, "This mission would be under your personal command?"

Borghese nodded. "The mission itself, yes — from the time we sail until we hit New York."

"And the overall command of the operation?"

"That will fall to the Duke of Alimone di Savoia — Admiral and nephew of the King."

"I see." The German regarded his guest closely for several long moments. Finally he spoke. "I like it," he said with a smile. "I'll give as much support as I can. For the present, and during your stay in Paris, please consider yourself a privileged officer on my staff. I'll take care of the details for that tonight.

"Next, I will arrange that you have access to my files and will provide officers to help you put together the information you need. In your handling of such material, I rely upon your good faith and judgement."

Borghese nodded. "I'll be discreet, Admiral. I'll not let you down. I appreciate your trust and your support."

"It sounds good!" said Doenitz. He broke into a warm smile. "As a matter of fact, it sounds great. So let's forget the wartime restrictions for the moment and have another bottle of wine to drink to success.

And one final question, Prince Borghese — When do you plan to make your attack?"

"At the most unexpected hour of them all ," Borghese replied. "At the perfect psychological moment — Christmas Eve, 1943."

Giorgio Giobbe,
E-boat commander.

Teseo Tesei, killed in
suicide attack at Malta.

Chapter 2.
Across Three Wars

For Borghese and his men to plan an attack on New York for 1943 meant drawing upon resources that had been a quarter of a century in their development — a span of years that embraced three wars.

It was on March 26, 1941, that the British cruiser *York* and three merchant ships had been sunk in a Light Flotilla attack on Suda Bay, near the northwest tip of Crete. Between that night and the hour of Italy's armistice agreement 30 months later, the men of the Tenth Light knocked out 31 ships of more than 265,000 tons aggregate. They injected a new and terrifying type of attack into modern naval warfare. They did so with such skillful success that the Mediterranean Sea, at the outset of 1942, hung like a ripe olive in the sun, ready to be plucked by the Axis powers; Great Britain and the United States would have been helpless to prevent it. Fortunately for the Allied cause, Hitler, in his blind ignorance of Naval strategy, failed to press home his advantage and thereby gave the Allies time to rush in their reserve strength and close the breach.

The weapons and the tactics with which the Tenth Light assaulted Mediterranean shipping in those days had their roots far back in the time of World War I. At the height of that distant conflict, Italy's prime challenge was a one-on-one struggle against the might of the Austro-Hungarian Empire. While bitter fighting raged on land and in the Alpine snows, Austria-Hungary maintained in readiness a power- ful fleet of heavy-gunned warships. These ships for the most part remained safely in harbor, behind the protection of mine fields and submarine nets. But always they represented a guillotine poised above Italy's neck. They were a menacing force that pinned down Italian defenses while threatening hourly to surge forth into the Adriatic Sea and ravage the Italian shores.

Italy's problem, therefore, was to invent and deploy a new weapon capable of breaking through the Austro-Hungarian harbor defenses and attacking the capital ships of the Imperial Fleet, particularly in the big Austrian anchorage at Pola.

The first attempt at solving this problem was a total failure. It was made by a Commander Pellegrini of the Italian Navy who penetrated the harbor at Pola with a crude form of amphibious assault craft. He called his vehicle the *Grillo*, the Italian word for cricket. But it was scarcely a nimble contrivance. It was simply a motorboat equipped with caterpillar treads, which theoretically would enable him to ride over nets and cables and carry an explosive charge to the flank of some targeted ship. Unfortunately for the Commander, he was spotted and captured by Pola lookouts one night as he tried unsuccessfully to crest the *Grillo* over the top of a mid-harbor barrier. He took a last home- ward look toward Italy and spent the rest of the war as a POW.

But then came two volunteers who were dogged enough and inven- tive enough to lick the problem. They were Navy Lieutenant Raffaele Paolucci, a young surgeon who later won international distinction in the medical profession, and Major Raffaele Rossetti of the Naval Engineers. (The Italian Navy designates its engineer officers by Army rank.)

Paolucci embarked on his project in February 1918. His plan was that he be carried by motorboat to a point about one mile from a gap in the Pola Harbor breakwater. "From that point," he said, "I'll swim with the special mine that I've invented and get to one of the *Radetzky* class of battleships that are anchored directly behind the defenses."

Paolucci's special mine was a torpedo-shaped weapon slightly over three feet long and two inches in diameter, supported by air tanks fore and aft and carrying a charge of 220 pounds of TNT. He proposed to suspend this beneath the targeted ship, activate a one-hour time fuse, and then withdraw.

"I'll simply retrace my route," he said. "I'll negotiate the defense nets again and, just outside, await the effect of the explosion. After it takes place, I'll swim further out to sea and, with my back to the enemy, flash a small electric torch to show the waiting motorboat where I am." Paolucci spent many months in rigorous nighttime training for his mission. Meanwhile Rossetti had been working since the beginning of the war on an intricate mine device of his own, a type of hand-steered torpedo called a *Mignatta*. He too was aiming for destruction of enemy fleet units in Pola Harbor. His proposal involved a compressed-air special torpedo, controlled by an external lever and capable of cruising at three or four knots with a range of eight or ten miles. It would carry a 350-pound charge of TNT, which would be attached to the hull of an enemy ship by a magnetic clamp or suspended beneath the hull on a 12-foot line.

The two inventors were eventually brought together when Captain Costanzo Ciano of the Italian Royal Navy was put in overall command of operations to penetrate Pola and promptly summoned both men for a pooling of ideas and energy.

"Paolucci," said Ciano, "stop your nighttime swimming and attack the problem with Rossetti. And Rossetti, stop your one-man programs and work with Paolucci. It's time we organized a team."

It proved to be a good combination. Working together. Paolucci and Rossetti came up with a crude but effective assault weapon. It consisted of a light motorboat with shallow draft and caterpillar treads, capable of riding over harbor nets as the *Grillo* was supposed to have done, and equipped to carry a powerful mine to the enemy target.

After many weeks of training and rehearsing, on the night of October 31, 1918, the two men set out from Venice on the torpedo boat 65PN, with Ciano in command. By evening they were at the mouth of the Pola Harbor. As darkness came down, they quietly launched their two-man assault craft, bade farewell to Ciano, and moved off toward the shadows of the enemy fleet.

By dawn on November 1, they had overcome vicious tidal currents and stubborn lines of defense nets, had reached their target, and had attached their mine to the hull of the huge battleship *Viribus Unitis*. Then, as quietly as they had entered the bay, they made their way back across the harbor to their waiting torpedo boat.

One hour later, as daylight broke, the Austrian dreadnought exploded in a tremendous roaring of flames and debris. A new type of guerrilla warfare had been born.

What further success the Italians might have had against the Austro-Hungarian ships will never be known, for at this point the march of diplomatic events got in the way. Ten days after the *Viribus Unitis* went to the bottom, Germany agreed to Armistice terms and the First World War came to an end.

For 17 years thereafter, Italy remained at peace and nobody bothered about improving the Paolucci-Rossetti Mignatta weapon nor about experimenting with new ones. But then, on October 2, 1935, Mussolini ordered the invasion of Ethiopia without bothering to declare war. This was an indirect challenge to the British to do something about it. And suddenly the Italian Royal Navy began to feel uneasy about its future well-being. What now? Would Britain declare war against Italy? If so, how could the Navy hope to survive?

As Borghese described it, in his chronicle of those days:

"How could Italy have resisted being overwhelmed by the crushing power and weight of the British fleet? In a war such as that to be expected, our chances would be discounted in advance. The disproportion of strength would be immense, both by sea and air. So, too, would be the inequality of industrial capacity and ability to maintain supplies. We should have been hemmed in within our small and cramped peninsula and bound to be starved into submission by the British blockade. How could we break out?

"And then an idea began to form in our minds: to create a destructive weapon and employ it unexpectedly and at the right moment, thus causing the enemy's fleet a substantial initial weakening by attacks launched during the first days of war.

"We required some kind of new, unforeseen weapon, rapidly produced and instantly employed, to carry destruction into the enemy's camp at the very start of hostilities. This would put us into position to face the conflict on terms of equal strength. The effectiveness of this weapon would be in its surprise value."

Into the picture then came two young officers from the Navy's submarine arm, Lieutenants Teseo Tesei and Elios Toschi, the former a man of sharp humor and robust build, the other a man of tall proportions and forthright speech.

They were the warmest of friends, alike in their love for the Navy and their passion for patriotism. They had studied together at the Naval Academy in the late 1920's. Toschi then had taken on advanced studies at the University of Genoa, and Tesei at Naples. Both were experienced deep-sea divers. As shipmates at the huge La Spezia naval base in northern Italy, they had long shared an interest in the early efforts of Paolucci and Rossetti and had often talked about the possibilities of developing the Mignatta into a top-quality assault weapon. Now at last, justified by the threat of war, they set out to design not only a better Mignatta but to develop it into a mobile weapon with which two men could approach and attack a target without ever showing themselves above the surface of the water.

Night after night, they worked together in close quarters at La Spezia, planning and charting, testing and figuring, until there came a day in late 1935 when they agreed that they had put together exactly the right ideas in exactly the right sequence for success.

The weapon that then took shape in their blueprints was something never before seen in naval armaments. In appearance, in size and shape, it looked like a 22-foot torpedo. Actually, it was a new type of submarine, powered by electricity and maneuvered by controls similar to those of an airplane.

What made it unique was the fact that its two-man crew would ride on the outside of their vehicle, one behind the other and in horseback fashion, with their faces protected from the water by air masks and curved plastic glass.

"At night," Toschi explained in his report, "under cover of darkness and steering by luminous control instruments, they will be able to aim at and attack their objective while remaining quite invisible to the enemy.

"The operators, unhampered by the steel structure, are free to move and act at will, to reach the bottom of the sea and travel along it in any way and direction, and are able to cut nets and remove obstacles with special compressed-air tools and, therefore, reach any target.

"Equipped with long-range underwater breathing gear, the operators will be able, without any connection whatsoever with the surface, to breathe and navigate under water at any depths up to 100 feet and carry a powerful explosive charge into an enemy harbor. Being utterly invisible and beyond the reach of the most sensitive acoustic detector, they will be able to operate in the interior of the harbor till they find the keel of a large ship, fashion the charge to it, and thus insure an explosion which will sink the vessel."

With no loss of time, they rushed their plans to the Naval Ministry at Rome for approval, at the same time requesting that two prototypes be built for early testing. Within one week, a favorable reply came back from Admiral Cavagnari, Chief of Staff: "Build them at once!"

And so, months later on a cold day in January, Toschi and Tesei astonished a gathering of Navy brass at La Spezia by mounting their weapon and disappearing into the chilly waters of the bay, maneuvering invisibly and at will, showing their heads above the surface only now and then briefly, to disappear and reappear again in a bewildering sequence of sprints and turns.

The test was a resounding success.

Said Toschi, "We felt a thrill of delight in the dark depths of the sea, where our tiny human-torpedo was behaving so obediently."

Chapter 3.
Assignment: Special Weapons

N ear the northern arc of the western coast of Italy, some 70 miles south of Genoa, the town of La Spezia looks out on the Ligurian Sea. It is a favored resort among the tourists. They return there again and again, to walk the roadways lined with oleander, to savor the shrimp and squid and mussel soup in the harborside restaurants, to visit the nearby shores of San Terenzo where Shelley dreamed his gentle dreams, and to enjoy the cliffside villages of Riomaggiore, Manarola, Corniglia, Vernazza and Monterosso al Mare, each with its own delicious wines. It is a place of charm and beauty.

But La Spezia is also a place of force and action, for it is the site of the most important naval base in Italy, and the mooring home for the heart of the Italian Navy's submarine fleet. It is also a laboratory for the research and development of new submarine assault weapons.

It was La Spezia, therefore, that the Navy selected in 1936 to be the working center for Toschi and Tesei in their proposed development of the new human-torpedo and other special weapons. This was where their model had been built and tested, this was where they should continue.

Supermarina, the nerve center of naval administration and operations in Rome, had been deeply impressed by reports of performance of the two-man torpedo, and excited by its untapped possibilities. A second demonstration, equally successful, was held later that same month in the presence of Admiral Falangola, who had been sent from Rome to make a personal assessment of the invention.

Falangola was delighted. The weapon was even better than he had been led to believe. It was, in a basic sense, the old Mignatta; but now it was so vastly improved and refined as to be in a category of its own.

This new Mignatta, he noted, could cruise for 12 hours at close to three miles an hour, with its crew either wholly submerged or with only their heads showing above the surface. It could descend to a depth of 120 feet, gaining ample clearance to pass under harbor obstructions or under the keel of any ship afloat. Its forward warhead was detachable and carried a payload of 600 pounds of TNT, easily removable underwater for affixing to a ship's hull. Its two operators, riding astride with their feet in stirrups, were equipped with all necessary gear from hermetic rubber suits and sabotage tools to underwater respirators cleverly designed to prevent air bubbles from surfacing.

Falangola was so enthusiastic, in fact, that after the second demonstration he donned a rubber suit and went into the icy black water to ride the torpedo himself, first with Toschi at the controls, and then with Tesei.

And that night over wine, talking with the two inventors in their quarters, he gave them the word that they had hoped to hear — the authority to keep on with their experiments, and to develop other special weapons as well.

"This one, now," said the Admiral, "this new Mignatta — What is its name?"

"Between ourselves we call it a human-torpedo," said Tesei. "Sometimes when it gets stubborn, we call it a pig."

Falangola shrugged. "Colorful, perhaps, but too undignified for the Navy's taste. It will probably go into the manual as the SLT, for slow-running torpedo."

"No objections," said Tesei. "It is still a human-torpedo."

"Call it what you like," the Admiral agreed. "The point is, its possibilities are staggering. I only wish that I could be young enough and brave enough to some day go into action with it. Tell me — how do you visualize the scenario of attack?"

Toschi leaned forward, his eyes shining, and began to talk.

"You see the dark outline of your target against the sky," he said. "You have dreamed of this moment for months. You have been training for it for years. This is the decisive moment. Success means glory. Failure, a unique opportunity lost forever.

"You move in at observation level — just your eyes above the surface of the water. You approach to within 30 yards of the target. There may be lights showing on deck. The flare of a match, or the sound of a song from the crew's quarters, may remind you that what you're about to destroy is something alive. But you cannot dwell on that. Instead you take a careful compass bearing. Then you flood the diving-tank, and the water closes over your head.

"As you submerge, everything is cold and dark and silent. Now you are deep enough. You close the flooding valve, put the motor into low gear and glide forward.

"Suddenly it gets darker — you are underneath the ship. Now you shut off the motor and open the valve for pushing the water out of the diving-tanks. As you slowly rise, you lift a hand above your head. You wonder whether it will touch smooth plates — or knife-edged barnacles that may rip your fingers or tear open your rubber suit and let in the sea.

"Now you have found the hull. You push the torpedo back, so that your assistant can grab the bilge keel which runs along each side of the underwater hull. You feel a thump on your shoulder — your assistant has found the bilge keel and is clamping a line on it. Two thumps on your shoulder — the clamp is in position.

"Now you go ahead to get at the bilge keel on the other side of the hull. Your assistant is paying out the line from one side to the other. He attaches the second clamp. Now back again, pulling yourself along by the line stretched under the hull.

"You reach the center of the ship. While you clutch the rope with both hands, gripping the torpedo between your legs, your assistant leaves his seat and moves past you till he reaches the warhead in front. In the darkness, you know that he is fastening the warhead to the rope stretched under the ship between the bilge keels. Now he has detached the warhead. It is in position. He sets the time fuse which will cause the TNT to explode in two and a half hours.

"The seconds begin to tick off. Your assistant returns to his seat. Three thumps on the shoulder — the job is done. You start the motor, glide away from under the ship and gently surface. Now you may think of escape."

Falangola beamed with satisfaction. "Exactly the way I picture it," he exclaimed. "It is precisely the weapon we need. It is our equalizer — against the British if they attack, or any other foe with naval power. But, one thing."

"Yes?" said Tesei.

"Secrecy. Above all, extreme secrecy. No government in the world must know about this until the right time — until the night, some night and somewhere — when we deploy it for action."

Toschi and Tesei nodded silent agreement.

"Now," said the Admiral, refilling his wine glass. "Here is how it shall be."

Toschi and Tesei leaned across the table, all attention.

"I have said you have the authority to continue," the Admiral went on. "But there are necessary conditions. You are to continue this work only when your regular duty schedules permit. You are to carry on your assignments in submarines as though nothing has happened here. We cannot spare talented men from normal duties right now, nor do we wish to risk drawing special attention to you. It would invite too many awkward questions.

"Unfortunately, that means there will be many days when you're absent from these parts, hundreds of miles away. Fortunately, though, orders will be arranged returning you to La Spezia more and more frequently as time goes on. And whenever you're back here, you will be working undisturbed on your special program. We expect you to develop still other assault weapons — not just the improved Mignatta. New torpedo boats, for example. New mining devices. If possible, a new one-man weapon of some sort. In other words, let your imaginations run free, and follow wherever they lead.

"The overall command for this program will go to Commander Catalano Gonzaga of the submarine flotilla. You all know each other, and he will work well with you. Other selected men of ideas will shortly be joining you — Lieutenants Franzini and Stefani, Midshipman Centurione, Guido Cattaneo for mechanical engineering, Commander Giorgis for construction.

"You will find that the Duke of Aosta has thoughts about linking your torpedo with air transportation for attacking distant harbors. His brother, the Duke of Spoleto, has proposals to offer about making a new explosive motorboat. These are good and loyal men — listen to their ideas. Perhaps you can blend them with your own."

The Admiral stood up to take his leave. He reached out with a warm handclasp for each man. "That is all for now," he said. "Your government is grateful — and perhaps will be even more grateful in the years ahead. None of us knows what awaits us in the future. It well may be that you gentlemen hold the fate of the Italian Navy in your hands. And as the Navy goes, so goes the fate of the nation. It's a terrible burden to carry, especially on the back of a human-torpedo. But you'll handle it well, I'm sure. Yes, very well indeed."

In the short space of the next few days, a new facility of the La Spezia submarine base began to take shape. It was located at the mouth of the nearby River Serchio, on the private estate of the Dukes of Salviati. It was far from any private road or prying eye. It was well hidden by tall, thick stands of pine trees that sloped majestically toward the shore of the sea. In the beginning, it was sheltered by a solitary tent. Then it expanded and moved into a vacant nearby farmhouse. Then it spread into newly constructed shops and laboratories. Only a handful of men knew of its existence. These were dedicated men, sworn to utmost secrecy, passionately devoted to their assignment and its purpose. They were creating what would some day become the Tenth Light Flotilla.

King Victor Emmanuel at a wartime meeting with Benito Mussolini

Chapter 4.
Rebirth at Serchio

On May 5, 1936, ranting pompously from the balcony of the Palazzo Venezia in Rome, Mussolini proclaimed Italy's total victory in East Africa and called off his troops. Ethiopia, he shouted, was now officially a part of the new Italian Empire. (Wild cheers from the crowd below.) King Victor Emmanuel, he bellowed, was henceforth an Emperor. From his allotted position in the background, the little King concurred. Britain made no move to interfere.

Thus barely 100 days after the River Serchio operation had swung into action, the irony of history shut it down. The war itself had evaporated. The few new assault weapons that had been developed were quietly stored away in hidden depots, and further technical research came to a limping halt.

But always, if one looks closely enough, there are wars or threats of war on the international horizon. And in the months that followed the dismantling of Serchio, the more perceptive leaders in the Italian Navy grew increasingly uneasy about the demands that might, some day soon, be made upon their fleet — and about the lack of special assault weapons to counter those demands.

Italy, for the moment, was at peace. True. But the world beyond Italy was beginning to writhe and seethe in the turmoil. Hitler's divisions had already goose-stepped into the occupied Rhineland, defying the rest of Europe to do anything about it. Civil war was raging in Spain, where the Loyalist Government had fled Madrid for Valencia, dodging bombs and shells every mile of the way. By March of 1937, British, French and German warships were warily patrolling the Spanish coasts. In the Far East, Japan was raping and pillaging the stronghold cities of China, taking time out in a moment of arrogance to bomb and sink the U.S. gunboat *Panay* in the shallow Yangstze River. In Berlin, Hitler tore up the Versailles Treaty and stabbed a finger at Austria as his immediate target for a takeover. It was clear, then, that sooner or later Italy would become one more ingredient in the boiling pot of violence; that sooner or later, Mussolini would feel impelled to start shouting again and join the saber-swingers.

Among those who foresaw the inevitability of involvement was Prince Borghese. He wrote of it in his journal:

"The swiftness with which the war in East Africa had ended in victory caused responsible military commanders to believe that the situation had improved and the threat of a European conflict was less imminent. Accordingly, the special weapons department had no sooner been set up than it was casually dissolved. This was a grave error. It was an error which should never have been committed, for the consolidation of our position in East Africa not only had failed to mitigate British enmity but actually had rendered it more positive, uncompromising and relentless."

But after two wasted years of inactivity at Serchio, with the world plunging headlong toward disaster, Supermarina finally stirred from its lethargy and decided to make ready for the inevitable. An order went out from Rome to a Commander Paolo Aloisi at La Spezia, appointing him to the command of what was then the First Light Flotilla, a little-known unit of very swift, maneuverable smallcraft. He was also directed to revive and take over the development of the special assault weapons.

Aloisi was an excellent choice for the job. He was an enthusiastic and talented leader with an avid interest in naval engineering. He immediately brought Guido Cattaneo back into the picture with orders to retrieve all the original Serchio plans and weapons, assemble a crew for research and development, and get on with the task of producing new improvements and inventions.

The results were swift and promising. In a short matter of months, the original Toschi-Tesei human-torpedo was upgraded and made more deadly and dependable than ever before. In addition, the new team came up with still another promising weapon, an explosive type of E-boat known as the MTM. This was a flat-bottomed, light-wood motorboat about 30 feet long and six feet wide, powered by an Alfa-Romeo 2500 engine that could drive it at a speed of 32 miles an hour. It was a one-man craft, so constructed as to glide over most defense nets without getting stuck. It carried in its nose an explosive charge of 600 pounds, set to detonate on impact or hydrostatic pressure against the hull of a ship.

The operator's duties were to pilot his boat over and around harbor defenses, take bow-aim on his targeted ship, shift to maximum speed, clamp the rudder onto true aim, and then eject himself and a small liferaft into the sea while his boat rushed to explode against the target. After that, it would be up to the operator to paddle his liferaft to safety, or escape, if possible. If he failed to make his getaway, the exchange would still be worthwhile: one man lost for one enemy ship destroyed.

Aloisi was delighted with the new product; and Supermarina was delighted with Aloisi. Thus in July of 1939, with an all-out war almost at hand, Aloisi received new orders from Rome

"The command of the First Light Flotilla is hereby entrusted with the duties of training a nucleus of personnel for employment with given special weapons, and of carrying out, under the general supervision of Admiral Goiran (Commander North Tyrrhenian Sector), experiments and tests concerned with the perfection of the said weapons."

At long last, then, after years of stop-and-go efforts, the Serchio project was about to come into its own. Thus, back to the pine-forest shores and the blue-green waters of the River Serchio, one by one, came the original group of Toschi, Tesei, Stefanini, Catalano and Centurione. As they began their special training in the handling of assault weapons, they were joined by new shipmates — men named De Giacomo, Di Domenico, Vesco, Birindelli, Bertozzi, de la Penne, and Aloisi himself.

To select and train the men of the assault teams, Supermarina recalled from retirement an ingenious old sea dog, Commander Angelo Belloni. He was well along in years and totally deaf, but he was the dean of all Italians in the field of submarine research and a long-time advocate of special insidious weapons.

The program that Belloni installed was the most demanding and selective in the entire Navy. Regardless of rank or rating, all candidates were put through the same trials and close scrutiny. They were checked not only for physical hardiness and their ability to remain underwater in chilling darkness for hours at a time but also for moral character, emotional stability and commitment to loyalty. Many of them were weeded out after passing the initial underwater tests; such men were quietly returned to their units as "certified expert breathing-gear divers." Those remaining were then admitted to the secret weapons division, but on a probationary basis only. At this point, their lives and backgrounds were probed and dissected with minute care. Their family antecedents were investigated. Their love affairs were studied. Their financial debts were scrutinized. Such characteristics as a quick temper, or impulsive over-betting on a hand of cards, in some cases would be considered reason enough for elimination from the program.

Commander Belloni, of course, always had the final word as to whether a man remained with the program. And Belloni also made the decision as to whether a man should enter an underwater unit, a surface-craft unit, or both, depending largely on the candidate's psycho-physiological traits.

Finally, all those who survived the careful weeding-out process were sworn to absolute secrecy regarding their work and their weapons. Not even a man's wife or parents were to be given any hint of the nature of the operation. Secrecy was so strict that not even the Italian manufacturers who produced the various parts for the weapons were allowed an inkling as to what they were involved in; it was their task simply to turn out their products and ship them to La Spezia, making certain that the bits and pieces of hardware bore no such clues as serial numbers or name of factory. This would make it almost impossible for enemy agents to trace a captured weapon to its source. The weapons were put together in final form by the trainees themselves, working day and night in the hidden sheds of River Serchio.

The end result was a variegated arsenal of secret assault weapons such as no Navy ever before had possessed.

There was the midget submarine known as the CA, a small 12-ton vessel designed for a two-man crew and two torpedoes. Its purpose was to enter an enemy harbor submerged and launch underwater saboteurs to mine enemy ships. It was joined, early on, by improved models known as the CA2 and the CB, the latter a 30-ton craft with a crew of four.

There was the SLC human-torpedo, an improved version of the original Toschi-Tesei weapon, designed to be carried on the deck of a standard submarine and launched near a harbor entrance.

There were the MTM explosive motorboats and an improved off-shoot, the MTR, also designed to be carried on submarines. There was the larger, twin-engine MTSM motorboat, a two-man craft equipped with torpedoes and depth charges and designed to operate in the open sea as well as in the confines of the harbor.

There were two types of special mines, the *Leech* and the *Limpet*, each designed to be carried underwater by a frogman and attached in quantity to a ship's hull. The *Leech* held a 4-pound explosive charge controlled by a time fuse. The *Limpet* held a 10-pound charge with a time fuse but was also equipped with a propeller-like apparatus that would explode the mine against a vessel's hull as soon as the ship attained a speed of five knots.

Not all of these weapons were ready for use when Italy entered the war against Britain and France on June 10, 1940. But they were on their way, and rapidly approaching operational capability. The dreams that had produced the base at River Serchio were about to produce a new type of warfare.

Submarine *Scire*, rigged to carry human-torpedoes.

Chapter 5.
Too Bold, Too Soon

On a summer's day in 1940, Commander Mario Giorgini sat behind a broad desk in his River Serchio headquarters and waited for his morning guest to be seated. Rising sunlight streamed through the window at his back and warmed the room. From outside came the subdued sounds of workmen's voices and busy machinery. Giorgini was gradually getting used to his secluded office. Scarcely a month earlier, he had been appointed by Rome to succeed Paolo Aloisi as head of the First Light Flotilla and to get involved with the special weapons program. He enjoyed his new surroundings. But he did not enjoy the prospect of carrying out the orders that had arrived from Rome the night before and that now lay on his desk. "We need more time," he complained to himself. "More time."

He waited until the five men he had summoned to his office had poured cups of coffee and seated themselves. He nodded appreciatively — they were a good group. Lieutenants Teseo Tesei, Elios

33

Toschi, Gino Birindelli, Alberto Franzini and Luigi de la Penne — the best officers in the special weapons program.

The Commander glanced from one to the other around the circle of faces. "All settled, gentlemen?"

"All settled." They nodded, and fell silent.

Giorgini lit a small cigar and gestured at the papers on his desk. "What I'm about to say may startle you," he said. "But these are my orders from Supermarina. And the orders involve you five."

The men waited expectantly.

"Air reconnaissance," he went on, "shows the presence of three British warships in the harbor at Alexandria. Three big ones. We have photographs of two battleships and an aircraft carrier at anchor. The carrier appears to be the Ark Royal. The others perhaps are the Queen Elizabeth and the Valiant. Or maybe the Barham. We're not positive of identification, of course, but the names are not important. What's important is that three big ships are sitting there — or were yesterday at this time. My orders are to knock them out."

The Commander paused, anticipating a response. When none was forthcoming, he continued his talk. "I plan to do this by using our five best human-torpedo teams, four for the attack and one team in reserve. Each of you will be assigned a trained petty officer diver to ride with you on your torpedo. The P.O. assignments are: — Alcide Pedretti to go with Tesei, Enrico Lazzari with Toschi, Damos Paccagnini with Birindelli, Emilio Bianchi with Franzini, and Giovanni Lazzaroni with de la Penne. The de la Penne team will be the reserve crew. Are there any questions so far?"

"Yes," said Tesei. "When is this to take place?"

The Commander nodded. "On the night of 25-26 August. At moonrise, about midnight. You will be transported to the harbor entrance by the submarine Iride. Any comments?"

"Yes'" said Toschi. "It's much too soon. We need more training. Some of our equipment has never been tested. And I'm afraid that Rome doesn't understand the delicate nuances of what we're trying to do. We could be in big trouble. What's the rush?"

"I agree with you," said Giorgini. "It is much too soon. Too early for our training to pay off properly and too early for the untested parts of our equipment. Unfortunately, Supermarina makes these decisions, not I. I suppose the reason they're rushing into this one is simply because the three big ships are there today and may not be there a month from today. I would prefer to spend much more time on training and equipment before attempting such a mission. In that respect I sympathize with you. But unfortunately there can be no delay on this one. The orders have arrived. They must be carried out."

Toschi shrugged. "It's premature. But we'll do our best."

"I know you will," said Giorgini. "Anything further before I go on? No? Very well, then — here's the way we'll proceed.

"The destroyer Calipso will take aboard the teams and the human-torpedoes at La Spezia and sail across to the coast of Africa, arriving at the Gulf of Bomba just west of Tobruk. Meanwhile the Iride, under command of Lieutenant Francesco Brunetti, will depart La Spezia and will join you at Bomba on the morning of August 21. There will be a supply ship there for refueling — probably the Monte Gargano.

"You will immediately transfer all your equipment from Calipso to the submarine. Your two-man torpedoes will be clamped into special chocks on the Iride's deck. Brunetti then will take his submarine out for one submersion test off the Gulf of Bomba just to make certain that everything is in working order, that the torpedoes stay in position. That test may be risky, by the way, for the water is shallow and very clear — ideal for getting spotted by some British patrol.

"With the test out of the way, the Iride will return to the bay and take you aboard and then will head for Alexandria on the evening of the 22nd. She will carry you to a point four miles off the harbor entrance, arriving on the night of the 25th. You will free your torpedoes and mount them for action. The Iride will then take leave of you and depart. And from then on, gentlemen, it's all up to you."

But Giorgini had guessed wrong; the outcome of the first Alexandria mission was never to be placed in the hands of the torpedo-men.

Both the *Iride* and the *Calipso* arrived at Bomba on schedule, gliding into the gulf within one hour of each other on the morning of the 21st. Gazing around from the deck of the destroyer, Toschi and Tesei and their shipmates looked out across a bleak setting of sea and landscape. Beneath them, the bay waters were crystal clear at a depth of 45 feet. In the near distance, turning slowly at anchor, rode the big Italian supply vessel *Monte Gargano*, flagship of Rear Admiral Bruno Brivonesi of the Libyan naval forces. Trawlers and small harbor-craft moved lazily about. At the far rim of the bay stood the stark sheds of a small Italian seaplane base. Beyond, the hot sand dunes of Africa lay parched in the sunlight.

"I don't like it," Franzini muttered, shaking his head. "I don't like it a bit. We stand out like ducks in a swimming pool."

Birindelli nodded agreement. "And with less room to operate. We can't fly up — the water's too shallow to go down — we're hemmed in on three sides by land. Whoever picked this place as a rendezvous, I recommend him for early retirement. He is unsafe for loyal sailormen."

Tesei shrugged. "Let's get the equipment transferred."

Some six hours later and without warning, moving in from the glare of a setting sun, three British aircraft swooped down on the distant seaplane base and dropped their strings of bombs. Two of the planes departed without further ado. The third one, though, stayed behind long enough to fly a broad, wary circle out across the bay and around the *Iride*, *Calipso* and *Monte Gargano*, much as to say, "Well, well! And what are those strangers doing down there? What in the world is going on?" Then it, too, climbed high, made a lazy turn and disappeared in the distance.

"That's it," said Toschi, watching the plane depart. "We'll have guests arriving in the morning, gentlemen — as surely as we'll have eggs for breakfast."

And Toschi was correct.

At 11:30 the next morning, three actions were taking place simultaneously. The *Calipso* had moored alongside the *Monte Gargano*, had transferred the 10 torpedo-men across for a courtesy visit, and was starting to refuel from the big supply ship. The *Iride*, with four human-torpedoes in their deck racks, had weighed anchor and was moving down the channel toward the mouth of the bay to carry out her submersion test. And seemingly from nowhere, three British torpedo planes suddenly were racing in to attack.

They swept in at low altitude, barely 200 feet above the sea, heading straight for the *Iride* in V-formation. Brunetti spotted them from the submarine's bridge and quickly gauged the channel's depth. No chance for an emergency dive.

"All ahead full!" he shouted. "Action stations! — Stand by to open fire!"

The planes dropped to 50 feet. Two of them roared by on either side of the *Iride*, raking her deck with deadly machine-gun fire. The third cut loose its torpedo in a bows-on shot that smashed home with a tremendous explosion. A gigantic column of dirty water leaped into the air. Bodies and debris splattered down. With a rumbling shudder, the broken *Iride* sank out of sight.

Without slacking speed, the planes veered sharply and tore across the bay for an attack on the *Calipso* and the *Monte Gargano*. On they raced, slamming through a storm of machine-gun fire that rose from the two ships. At 200 yards out, one plane launched a torpedo that plunged into the sea and went foaming past the *Calipso*, a near miss. The *Calipso* promptly cut her moorings and struggled to break free. A moment later, a second torpedo hit the sea and rushed toward the *Monte Gargano*. The men from River Serchio, standing helpless on the deck, watched its approach in stricken fascination. With a shattering roar, the torpedo struck home and the ship exploded.

Bodies, wreckage and gouts of oil shot into the air and splashed back to the sea in a screaming, bloody shower. Toschi, hurled overboard, floundered up from the depths while debris was still raining down. He gasped for breath and tested his limbs. He was unhurt. So were his team-mates, all of them now struggling to stay afloat in the seething confusion. Tesei was close by. So was Birindelli. And Franzini. Miraculously, they had all survived. One by one, and helping each other through the swirling wreckage, they fought their way to *Calipso*'s side and were taken aboard. For the moment at least, for them the worst was over.

A quick glance back at the *Monte Gargano* showed all too plainly that nothing could be done to save the big ship. She was listing sharply to port, threatening to capsize even while sinking. Already a dozen harbor-craft and trawlers were speeding to the scene to rescue survivors.

Aboard *Calipso*, the ship's telegraph rang for full ahead, and the destroyer began racing toward the spot where the *Iride* had disappeared. Within ten minutes, Brunetti and six shipmates, oil-smeared and bleeding, had been pulled from the sea, and the *Calipso* had located the shattered submarine on the channel bottom. She lay on her side in 50 feet of water, pouring out oil, broken in two at the level of her gun position. There was no sign of life; 44 men were unaccounted for.

Using spare bits of diving equipment, the men from River Serchio dove from *Calipso*'s deck again and again, plunging into the depths to try to determine what chance there might be for rescue efforts — assuming any submariners were left alive. But the chance was not promising. The officers' quarters had been completely flooded; no man who had been trapped there could have survived. A close examination of the broken hull offered little hope that anyone remained alive within. Only the *Iride*'s flag, still in position, stirred eerily in the water. Discouraged, the divers called off their efforts for the time being, to await the arrival of special salvage and rescue equipment being rushed to the scene from the Italian base at Tobruk.

When diving resumed a few hours later, however, hope rose almost immediately. It was Tesei, diving alone, who made his way excitedly to the surface with news that men were still alive in the wreckage.

"They're in the after torpedo compartment!" he cried. "I heard their voices! I rapped on the hull and they returned my signals!"

Back to the wreck went Tesei, with Toschi diving by his side. To their astonishment, they discovered they could not only hear and understand the voices of the trapped men, but by pressing their face masks directly against the hull they could even carry on an underwater conversation.

"How many are in there?"

"Nine. For God's sake, please help us!"

"We'll help. What's it like in there?"

"All black. Can't see a thing. We're partly flooded."

"Do you need fresh air?"

"Yes — badly. We can smell chlorine gas."

"How about the escape hatch?"

"No good. It jammed in the explosion."

"Hang on. We'll find a way to get you out."

For the next 20 hours, then, working without rest, the men from River Serchio struggled to free the jammed hatch. Finally, at dawn the following day, with the aid of a strong windlass on the *Calipso*, they pulled the steel trap free. Suddenly a way was open for the men to escape.

Toschi and Tesei went down again and rapped on the hull plates. This time the response was weak.

"Can you hold out just a little longer?"

"Not long," came the reply. "Two men died last night."

"Listen carefully now." Tesei ordered. "We're ready to get you out. But you must do exactly as I say. You must open your watertight door — flood the whole compartment. Hold on tight against the rush of water pouring in. Then swim underwater to the escape hatch and come to the surface. You must act very quickly. Understood?"

The response was silence, then a long murmur of voices in conference. At last, "No, sir — we won't do it."

Tesei swore in exasperation. After so much work! "You must do it! It's the only way!"

"No, sir. We're not going to open the door. We'd rather die here in peace than be drowned by water rushing in."

Tesei remained silent for several moments, wondering how best to cope with men who were being driven half-mad with fear. The only way to persuade them to act, he decided, was to pretend to be callous and cold.

"Listen here!" he demanded. "Do you hear me?"

"We hear you."

"Then you'll do as I say, or die where you are. I've told you exactly what to do. You have my last instructions. This is the last time I'll speak to you. We're going to leave you now and return to the surface. We'll wait there for exactly half-an-hour. If you haven't obeyed my orders and come up by then, we'll sail away and leave you. That is all."

Without another word, the two divers moved away from the hull. They paused, then, only long enough to retrieve the *Iride*'s flag. Then they shot upwards and returned to *Calipso*, leaving silence in the watery depths behind them.

Back on the *Calipso*'s deck, the Serchio men stood mute, staring fixedly at the blue expanse of water, watching for the telltale swirl that would show them the hatch had been opened. For long, slow minutes nothing happened. The half-hour ticked along and neared its end. Then suddenly, with a roaring rush, a column of water and turbid waste shot out of the sea and fell back with a resounding splash.

"They've opened it!" Tesei shouted.

A shrill, agonizing cry split the air. One man shot up from below, breaking water just off the port bow, spilling waist-high above the surface. Then another..and another..another....

One by one, the trapped submariners came floundering back into the sunlight and fresh air and a chance to go on living. And with the last of the seven finally aboard, *Calipso* turned slowly down the harbor channel and picked up speed along a course leading back toward La Spezia. It had been a tragic beginning for the torpedo teams. The losses were severe — one submarine, one supply ship, at least 100 men.

And as the destroyer moved out to sea, Commander Giorgini stood alone at the stern rail, staring back along the ship's wake to where the scene of disaster was fading in the distance. He bit hard on his unlit cigar and fought down his inner anger. Toschi had been right — they had gone out much too soon. It had all been such a waste.

Italian destroyer *Crispi*, transported E-boats to Suda Bay area.

Self- exploding E-boat, type used at Suda Bay and Malta.

Chapter 6.
Borghese Comes
Aboard

One week after the *Calipso* got back to La Spezia, Prince Borghese arrived at the base from a tour of duty in northern waters. He had been operating out of the German submarine school at Memel, on the Baltic Sea. There, since mid-summer, he had been cruising aboard U-boats while taking Admiral Doenitz' special training course for submarine warfare against North Atlantic convoys. By all logic his next assignment should have been to take command of an ocean-going Italian submarine operating out of Bordeaux.

But Supermarina had other plans for Borghese. Those plans had been broached to him by a representative of the Rome ministry upon Borghese's departure from Memel.

"You may join the Battle of the Atlantic if you wish. You've earned that right, and we would not stand in your way. However, Doenitz is doing very well out there without your help. We'd prefer you to accept a more important role and a much more challenging assignment."

Borghese waited, curious. "Tell me."

"Your background could not possibly be better applied than for what we have in mind. You've served on several submarines?"

"Nine of them," Borghese replied.

"Right. And you've commanded one of your own."

"The *Vettor Pisani*. A leaky old tub out of Sicily."

"You're the Navy's best underwater navigator. And you know every shoal and current in the Mediterranean."

Borghese shrugged. "Sometimes I think they change every week."

"And you're aware of what's going on at River Serchio."

He felt a rush of excitement. "I'm aware that it's the most important program in the Navy."

"Yes. Well now, what we plan to have you do..."

So on a soft August evening, Borghese had arrived dockside at La Spezia and stood gazing with enthusiastic pride at his new command, the submarine *Scire*. She was moored alongside a sister craft, the submarine *Gondar*. Each was a small, sleek Mediterranean-type vessel of 620 tons. Each was equipped with the most modern of navigational and control instruments. Ton for ton, they were probably the best submarines in the Italian fleet. Each had been converted from a standard submarine design to a new form befitting her special mission as an "assault craft transport." For this purpose, the deck guns on each craft had been removed to help make room for three bulky steel cylinders, one forward and two aft, each designed to carry underwater one of the two-man torpedoes from Serchio.

Borghese noted with approval that the *Scire*'s conning tower had been narrowed and cut back, to diminish its size as a surface target. And the vessel had been painted a deceptive shade of pale green, upon which was over-painted the silhouette of a trawler which seemed to be heading in a direction opposite that of the submarine, a tricky bit of camouflage almost certain to confuse a sighting enemy. Borghese liked what he saw.

He was still immersed in critical admiration of his vessel when a movement aboard the *Gondar* caught his eye. Stepping out on deck was his friend and former shipmate Francesco Brunetti.

Brunetti paused, greeting Borghese with a shout and a wide salute. "Valerio! I hear she's yours!"

"Right!" Borghese called back. "And the Gondar? She's yours?"

"All mine." Brunetti gave a sweep of his arms. "But why are we shouting? We've got a lot to talk about. Come aboard and let's have a drink."

It was on a night nearly three weeks later when the two submarine commanders requisitioned a staff car and drove south down the coast toward River Serchio. Their trip was being made in response to a summons from Commander Giorgini; he planned to hold a briefing session at midnight. Orders had arrived from Supermarina.

The drive itself, made gentle by a warm summer breeze and the scent of coastal pine trees, was a pleasant release from the monotony of assault-craft training. Night after recent night had been spent in rehearsing the intricate pattern of bringing a submarine undetected to the mouth of a harbor and of launching the underwater attack teams. From the *Scire* and from the *Gondar*, alternating in one practice session after another, the Serchio men had been slipping in and out of La Spezia's bay, challenging the lookouts and defensive units of their own navy to catch them in the act of "attacking" a ship. Just the previous night, the underwater torpedo teams had "sunk" the Italian battleship *Giulio Cesare* and the cruiser *San Marco*, much to the frustration of the deck crews. Elsewhere, the surface-craft drivers had been equally busy, probing with their motorboats by night along the blacked-out Ligurian coast, practicing their landings and harbor attacks under conditions close to those of enemy contact. All in all, the work was coming along nicely.

And now there would be this meeting with Giorgini which, as both men knew, meant only one thing: orders for an assault on live targets, on the unsuspecting ships of the English.

Brunetti was at the wheel of the car, guiding it smoothly along the dark, curving highway that skirted the Ligurian Sea. Beside him, Borghese was in a philosophic mood, talking quietly and reflectively about the nature of their work and the men with whom they were training.

"You know, Francesco," he said. "We are fortunate to be serving with such a group."

"We are indeed," said Brunetti. "They're the best. You should have seen them at Bomba. Blown into the sea one moment, diving to the rescue of others the next. Courage and guts to spare."

"They have class," Borghese went on. "A special style of their own. Picture them as they were two nights ago, just after they'd 'sunk' the San Marco for about the fifth time. There we were, all together in the ship's wardroom. Officers, petty officers, seamen — all sitting side by side and enjoying our bowls of hot pasta. Some of the men were still shivering, still cold from all those hours under the sea. The crease-marks of their masks were still on their faces. Their fingertips were still white and wrinkled from being under water so long. Nobody complained."

"Nobody ever does."

"They have big hearts," said Borghese. "And steel muscles, and lungs that can stand almost anything. In their own quiet way, they're quite magnificent. And I like their approach to their work — their self-appraisal. For example, take that curly-haired blonde giant, de la Penne. He'd made a perfect run with his human-torpedo that night. But then he came to me in the wardroom and asked, 'How did it go today, boss? We do O.K.?' And before I could answer, Birindelli — the silent Tuscan — he broke in and said, 'We'll have to do better!' Then Tesei spoke up: 'We'll do better at Malta. But we'll be doing our best only when we blow ourselves sky-high — when we die at our task.' And you know, Francesco? — I believe he means it."

"I'm sure he does," said Brunetti, "He's a zealot."

"So then," Borghese went on, "up spoke Martellotta with just four words: 'Peace and good will.' And everybody nodded gravely and went back to eating macaroni. They're quite a crew."

"True," said Brunetti, watching the road "What motivates them, do you suppose?"

Borghese was silent a moment. Then, "I don't know, exactly. They're all volunteers, of course. They've volunteered for a high-risk program that has already killed some of their shipmates. They feel sorrow for those deaths, but not depression. Each man knows that it may be his turn to die tomorrow. He accepts that chance, but so do many others in the Navy.

"So what makes these men so different from their fellows? — so indifferent to personal and material interests, so mentally and philo-sophically superior to the average man? It's not ambition. They're not seeking praise or decorations. It's not wealth, for there's no special monetary reward in what they do. It can't be a desire for professional promotion, for they could win that a lot quicker at a desk in the Ministry than by swimming around at the bottom of the sea. It's not common vanity or a desire to be known as heroes — for scarcely anybody knows who they are, and not even their wives or sweethearts know what they're doing.

"I suppose," he went on, "it is one faith alone that inspires them — a faith in their readiness and willingness, as Italian Navymen, to give themselves entirely to the service of their country. With no reservations whatever. Their offering is total and absolute. In them, it is an instinctive element, and the very essence of what we call patriotism. In its pure form, it is a very rare thing to possess. And that's what makes them such a remarkable group of men."

"Well put," said Brunetti.

The car sped south, purring along past blacked-out villas and seaside cottages, past curves of white-sand beach that showed dimly and fleetingly in the darkness, across ancient stone bridges that spanned small creeks, past rows of tall pine trees that stood like shadow-sentinels beside the road. It was a good night for driving. Peaceful and still. There were no reminders of war, except for the blackout darkness and the occasional stab of a searchlight probing out across the bay. Borghese lit a cigarette and leaned back, enjoying the ride and letting his mind travel ahead to thoughts of River Serchio and what it was like to live there.

Today's schedule would have been an easy one, he reflected. There would have been a chance for the men to rest up after the hard training duties of the past week. Some of the crew probably would have stayed in their quarters, lolling on their bunks, studying aerial photographs and maps of the enemy harbors at Alexandria and Malta and Gibraltar and Suda Bay, studying the patterns of docks and mooring-places and defensive barriers which they already knew as well as a man knows his own bedroom in the dark. And they would have studied also the silhouettes and characteristics of enemy warships, impressing them to memory so clearly as to be able to recognize and identify them instantly, even in the shadows of deepest night.

And others? Some, he reflected, would have been outside playing volley ball or tennis. Some would have gone on long quiet walks through the woods. Some would have spent their time at the shore, swimming and sun-bathing. Some would have gone hunting, tracking down the huge wild boars that roamed the Salviati game preserves. And perhaps, that evening, some would have gathered around a fire by the side of the river to sing old songs and sea shanties — and new ones too, like the song they had composed for British seamen, and had set to the tune of an old Italian folk song.

He groped in his mind for a moment, searching for the words and melody. Then it came clear to him, and he began to sing. Brunetti joined in, and they sang in harmony as the car sped along through the night:

"Hello, Jack Tar! What a beautiful day!
We frogmen are coming to teach you to swim,
So we hope you're in shape, we hope you're trim.
We dive, then you go down to stay.
So drop your bombs, drop them galore,
Drop them from aft and drop them from fore!
We dive, then you go down to stay.
Farewell, Jack Tar! What a pitiful day!"

Borghese glanced at the luminous face of his wrist watch. Another ten minutes and they'd be there. River Serchio lay close ahead, just around the next curving hill.

He patted his jacket pocket, casually touching the envelope that contained his orders. This would be a good one: simultaneous attacks at each end of the Mediterranean — on Gibraltar and Alexandria, each at the same hour.

Chapter 7.
Mission West, Mission East

"The attacks will be synchronized," Commander Giorgini was saying to the men. "They will take place at the extreme ends of the Mediterranean on the night of 29-30 September. As of tonight, each of the two harbors holds a full complement of British warships. Supermarina believes they will still be there when we arrive."

It was well after midnight. The group in Giorgini's briefing room at Serchio sat around in informal comfort, absorbing the details of the two-headed mission. Most of them had shed their uniform jackets and were relaxing in their shirt sleeves, smoking cigarettes and sipping wine. Thumb-tacked to the wall in front of them were detailed sketches of the distant harbors showing battleships, cruisers and aircraft carriers at anchor. A warm pre-dawn breeze came through the open windows, carrying the scent of salt water and pine needles into the room.

"For each targeted harbor," Giorgini said, "there will be four of our human-torpedo teams — three for attack and one in reserve. Borghese will take the Scire and carry an eight-man group to Gibraltar, pausing at La Maddalena for a final departure check. Brunetti, with the Gondar, will take the Alexandria group aboard at Villa San Giovanni in the Strait of Messina, then proceeding to Tobruk for a departure check. I will accompany the Alexandria group. In each case, the submarine will surface near the enemy's harbor entrance at 2030 hours on the 29th and await last-minute radio instructions from Rome. Now for the assignments."

The Commander placed his braided cap upside down on the desk before him. "This is our lottery bowl," he explained. He tossed a handful of small cards into the upturned cap. "Eight name-cards," he said. "One for each of you torpedo-men. We'll draw now to see which men go to Gibraltar and which go to Alexandria — and you'll get your Petty Officer assignments later.

"But before I draw, I have one stipulation to make: Toschi and Tesei must go in opposite directions. They know more about the human-torpedo than all the rest of us put together. Ergo, we divide their brain power — half for Gibraltar, half for Alexandria. The first one to be drawn goes to Alexandria. Everybody ready?"

"Ready," came from the men.

Giorgini stirred the cards around in his cap and lightly bounced them up and down. He stared out across the room and reached in blindly. He picked out a card, glanced at it, and placed it face up on the desk.

"It's Toschi," he announced. "Alexandria for you, Elios."

"Suits me." Toschi shrugged.

"And that means Gibraltar for you, Teseo." Giorgini reached into the cap again. "Franzini, to Alexandria — next, Birindelli to Gibraltar — Stefanini, you get Alexandria — de la Penne, to Gibraltar — finally Calcagno, reserve team for Alexandria — and Bertozzi, reserve team for Gibraltar. And that's that. See me tomorrow about selecting your Petty Officer crewmen. And good luck to all of you." He rose quickly, picked up his cap and strode from the room.

The men pushed back their chairs and shuffled to their feet. They mingled briefly, commenting in low voices on the luck of the draw, and then began drifting into the night to make their way to their

quarters. Borghese and Brunetti walked along with them, each drawing around him the men he would carry on the mission.

As they neared their quarters, Toschi said a quiet "Good night,
Francesco" to Brunetti and then moved through the shadows to the
side of Tesei.

"I don't feel like sleeping, Teseo," he said. "Will you walk with
me?"

Tesei turned away from his group. "I was about to ask you the same
thing," he said. "Let's go down by the river. Who knows when we'll
get another chance?"

They made their way along the path, walking softly on the thick
carpet of pine needles. The breeze made gentle rustlings in the
branches above them. Nearby, an owl hooted in the darkness, and
from the far distance came the high, thin bark of a wandering fox. The
men reached the riverbank and followed the shore far downstream
until they came to a flat rock overhanging the water. There they sat
down and took out cigarettes. The flare of Toschi's lighter shone
briefly in the pool below. After a while, he spoke.

"I feel uneasy, Teseo," he said. We've been the best of friends and
had good times together. But now, tonight, I'm troubled about what's
ahead."

"Troubled about the mission?" He sounded perplexed. "It's what
we've been wanting for several years, isn't it? But I think I know what
you mean. Lots of things could go wrong."

"Perhaps," said Toschi. "Perhaps not. It isn't the mission itself that
concerns me, though. It's what may happen to you."

"Elios," Tesei protested. "Either of us may die at any time. I'm as
concerned about you as you are about me. Perhaps more so right now,
because you're going to Alexandria and I'm going to Gibraltar. It
won't be difficult to get home from Gibraltar, with the help of our
friends in Spain. But it will be almost impossible for you to get home
from Alexandria."

Toschi shrugged. "It's not that. It's your indifference to death. You
are going one way and I am going another, and perhaps we'll never see
each other again. I can accept that if it's inevitable. But I can't accept a
death that's unnecessary. A man should try his best to stay alive."

"I'm not indifferent to death," Tesei said quietly. "On the contrary,
I think it's my duty to die."

"And that," said Toschi, "is exactly what I mean — that is just
what troubles me. It is not your duty to die. It's your duty to stay alive,

and if anybody has to die let it be the enemy. Sometimes you've said to me, 'Elios, you will survive but I will not — I intend to give my life.' That is wrong, Teseo. It is wrong for a man to kill himself when he has a chance to save himself. It is life that is important, not death."

"No, Elios," Tesei shook his head slowly from side to side. "No, I think not. I feel very strongly about this — that it is not important who wins a battle — it is not even important who wins this war. The important thing, my friend, is to die for your country. Nothing else matters. Nothing at all."

Toschi sighed. After long minutes of silence, he got to his feet. He reached down and took Tesei's hand and pulled him up. "Let's go back and get some sleep," he said. "The sun will soon be up. God has given us another day for living. Sometime, give a thought to how generous He is being."

Twilight shadows were beginning to cloak La Spezia on the evening of 21 September when Brunetti eased the *Gondar* out of its slip and set a southward course for the Strait of Messina. There, three days later at 5 o'clock in the morning, he was to rendezvous with a tender off the coast of Villa San Giovanni and take aboard Giorgini and the eight men chosen for the Alexandria torpedo crews, all of whom were making the journey to Messina by rail.

The rendezvous was carried out smoothly.

"Our express train rushed southwards," Toschi wrote in his journal the next day. "We spent our time reading newspapers and smoking. From time to time, Giorgini stopped reading and stared fixedly out of the window.

"I watched him from the corner of my eye, trying to share his thoughts. Then our glances met. He laughed and pretended to go on with his newspaper, but it was obvious that nobody was paying any attention to what he was supposed to be reading; each of us was running over in his mind all the preparations that had been made for us to penetrate the harbor at Alexandria. Each felt an inward thrill, anticipating the moment of the explosion beneath the keel of an enemy ship.

"Each of us carried only one small suitcase, containing what we should need for a few days only, for the time to reach Alexandria. Nothing was taken along for a return journey, for there would not be one; we would die or we would be taken prisoners.

"At the end of the line, when I stepped from the train into the fresh, damp air of the night, I reminded myself that we were travelling to Egypt on a journey from which there could be no return. We were going to visit the enemy in his most heavily fortified stronghold, on an errand of war and destruction only. The idea that we were not going to return gave me a momentary pang — my native land, the soil of which I was then treading, had never seemed so dear to me.

"The tug was waiting for us in the little harbor. We went aboard, and a few minutes later were alongside the Gondar, which had arrived some hours earlier. We had no sooner embarked than her two engines started up with a deafening roar and the submarine moved off at a gathering speed, taking a course southwest. Brunetti, remembering the fate of the Iride, was in no mood for unpleasant encounters by daylight in shallow and narrow waters. He did not intend to waste a second in getting out to where he could submerge.

"Personally I felt fit and at ease. I had taken leave of my family, and now I had said farewell to my country. There were no other ties for me to break. I had nothing more to lose."

And as the Gondar was moving south, the Scire had slipped silently out of La Spezia with the Gibraltar torpedo teams aboard. Borghese's initial course lay due south, sailing down between Elba and Corsica to put in at La Maddalena on the northeastern tip of Sardinia.

There he paused to make radio contact with Rome for his final departure instructions. They came crackling through the night exactly on schedule, and he nodded approvingly as he read them over his radio operator's shoulder. If all went well, he was to take the Scire into the Bay of Algeciras and select a suitable point for the launching of the attack on Gibraltar. The human-torpedoes were to attack such targets as Borghese would indicate in accordance with last-minute wireless information to be received from Rome. The order of precedence in selecting targets would be: battleships, aircraft carriers, cruisers, occupied docks. On escaping from the harbor, the torpedo crews were to rendezvous at specific points on the Spanish shore, where they would be picked up by friendly agents and returned to Italy by air.

The message from Rome came to an end. Borghese spoke briefly to his operator — "Acknowledge." Then he summoned his navigation officer and stepped to the submarine's chart table to lay out a course that would bring him to the coast of Spain on the evening of the 29th.

And on that evening, at the other end of the Mediterranean, the Gondar surfaced at a point six miles off the entrance to Alexandria harbor to await final instructions for attack. Toschi joined Brunetti on the bridge, and the two men carefully scanned the waters around them. The sea seemed deserted. Yet, this close to the enemy base, there was always the chance that a destroyer or some other patrol craft might be lying in wait a short distance away, listening with detectors, ready to pin down an intruder and race in for the kill. It was a dangerous place to be sitting.

Brunetti paced back and forth nervously, chafing with impatience for the signal from Rome. He glanced at his watch. The time was now; the word should be coming. What was the delay?

At that moment, the ship's duty officer came scrambling up from below with the message in hand.

"Sir! Received from Rome!"

Brunetti read it quickly and swore. He handed it to Toschi. The two stared at each other, speechless with frustration and anger.

"*British fleet has left harbor*," said the coded message. "*Return to Tobruk.*"

Brunetti shook off his disgust and disappointment. He prepared to put about and head back along the course to Tobruk. He stepped to the talk-pipe and called down to the engine room. "Starboard engine ahead one-third — port ahead one-third — both engines ahead half."

As the *Gondar* turned and began to straighten out, he took a final look around at the darkening surface of the sea. Then he froze. Looming out of the shadows, barely 800 yards off the port quarter, he saw the foaming bow of an onrushing British destroyer, bearing down directly on the submarine.

"Dive! Dive! Dive!" Brunetti shouted down the tube.

The klaxon sounded. In the rush of an instant, the men cleared the bridge and scuttled down the ladder, slamming the hatch tight behind them.

Chapter 8.
Scuttled Hopes

The *Gondar* plunged down at a sharp angle, hurling men and loose equipment to the deck of the control room. Toschi grabbed a handrail to hold himself upright.

"Did they see us?"

"I don't know," Brunetti told him. "We'll find out in a moment. They're heading right at us." He stared at the depth gauge, tracking the submarine's descent. Down 100 feet...down 150...down 200....

"Level off at two-five-oh," he ordered.

At that depth, the *Gondar* straightened out, cut engines, and hung suspended in watery silence. The crew waited in suspense, standing motionless, guarding against any telltale noise that might be detected by the destroyer on the surface. Then, faintly at first but swiftly growing louder, on came the sound of twin propellers approaching overhead at high speed. The men braced themselves. The rushing sound passed directly above them.

An instant later five violent explosions, one right after another, hammered the submarine and sent men and gear sprawling. The *Gondar* reeled and lurched under the shock. All lights went out, plunging the ship into utter blackness. The crash of breaking glass mingled with the creaking of strained plates and rivets. In the wake of the attack, the emergency lights flickered on and off, stayed on. The sound of the propellers faded, receding in the distance. The men breathed more easily, and the *Gondar* came alive again.

"Damage reports!" Brunetti ordered. "Quick now!"

One by one, from beyond watertight doors, the crews in other compartments reported to the control room by telephone. The damage was not serious. Glass and lights had been smashed. No critical instruments had been destroyed. Several air valves had lost their metal pins, cut through by sheer strain. One propeller-shaft housing had sprung a small leak. But the *Gondar*'s hull itself had come through in good shape. For the moment at least, they were safe.

With engines and instruments all silenced, the submarine dropped slowly, down and down, until Brunetti leveled her off at 400 feet. He held her there for long, nerve-wracking minutes. The men, seated or squatting at their stations, listened apprehensively for the dreaded sound of an enemy detector beam bouncing off the hull. And then it came, faint and high-pitched. And again, louder. And then again, at regular, persistent intervals, each time sounding closer and more distinct.

Brunetti grimaced. They had been tracked down. "Report," he ordered softly.

"Ship approaching at three-two-oh," came the reply. "Drawing nearer...Number Two strength...Two more ships joining...Number Three strength...Coming close...Three ships...."

Brunetti shook his head desperately. "All ahead full!"

The *Gondar* lunged forward with a shudder. But she moved too late. Five hammering explosions slammed against her again, shaking her compartments with a thundering roar, knocking the vessel about like a sea bird caught in a hurricane. Men picked themselves up from the deck, as the propeller sounds faded away. And this time, the damage reports were ominous. A bad leak in the engine room, a bad leak in the after torpedo room, water hissing down from the overhead plates, water pressing in through shorn rivets. The vessel swayed, rocked and dipped, almost out of control, dropping foot by foot toward the sea bed.

"All pumps!" said Brunetti. "Get her in trim."

From then on, through the long, agonizing hours of the night, the three attacking ships kept up their hammering assault. The *Gondar* twisted, climbed, shot down again, reversed course, and tried in every possible way to outmaneuver her attackers and escape. But nothing worked. She was pinned in a relentless detector fix, and brought under attack over and over again. Meanwhile her pumps were barely able to keep up with her leaks. And each new onslaught drove her lower and lower toward the critical 500-foot mark where sea pressure alone might crush her to pieces.

At 8 o'clock in the morning, after a night of agonizing horror, the submarine's depth gauge stood at an alarming 508 feet. The hull plates were screeching and groaning under the strain. Total collapse seemed only moments away.

Brunetti hurriedly called a conference of his key officers, with Giorgini and Toschi sitting in.

"We'll have to put an end to it," he said. "We can do no more. Our time has run out. Giorgini, you're in command of the mission. What's your word on our final move?"

"You're in command of the ship," Giorgini said. "I do as you say."

"Toschi? You speak for your men."

Toschi nodded. "As Mario just said, you're running the ship. You lead, we follow."

"Very well, gentlemen. And thank you." Brunetti paused, glancing from one to the other. "Now then, here's the situation," he said. "Above all, we must keep the secret weapons — the torpedoes — out of British hands. We can do that very easily just by staying here, for the ship will break up in a matter of minutes. But if we do that, it means death for every man aboard. Our other choice is to surface, if we can. We've barely enough compressed-air left to take us up — perhaps yes, perhaps no. But I think we should try. If we can surface, we may be able to scuttle the ship before the British spot and seize the torpedoes — and let's hope to God the enemy rescues some of us before killing us all

"So up we go, and pray we make it! Now if you'll excuse me, I'll get everything ready to scuttle."

Minutes later, in a surging roar, the last of the compressed-air supply went rushing into the vent tanks. In the control room, every man's stare was fixed on the depth gauge. Life or death hinged on whether the needle moved. Then suddenly, the *Gondar* shivered, shaking herself like an animal roused from sleep. The needle stirred, flickered, began to move. And slowly, slowly, the ship began to rise, gathering momentum each foot of the way, going up and up, until at last she burst the surface of the sea like a giant air bubble. She lay there rolling heavily from side to side as torrents of water poured down from her flanks.

Instantly, hatches slammed open. The men scrambled out on deck, blinking in the brilliant sunlight, filling their lungs with great gulps of pure, salt air.

Brunetti clambered to the conning tower bridge. "Abandon ship!" he shouted. "Abandon for scuttling!"

Men hurled themselves into the sea, floundering desperately to get away from the sinking boat. A rain of gunfire poured in on the *Gondar* from three directions. Two British destroyers and a corvette, all within 300 yards of the submarine, raked the stricken vessel with round after round of shellfire and turned their machine guns on the swimming survivors. As if that weren't enough, a Sunderland bomber came diving out of the sky, swooped to within 100 feet of the sea and dropped a deadly string of depth charges. Men screamed in agony, as the bombs exploded above and around them.

Toschi, struggling clear of the conning tower hatch, flung himself overboard and began to swim frantically toward the nearest ship. An underwater explosion dealt him a smashing blow in the stomach and threw him waist-high out of the water. Through blurred eyes, he saw the *Gondar* rising higher and higher out of the sea, rearing up for the death plunge. In another instant she was gone, knifing down in a great foaming swirl, carrying the torpedoes with her.

Toschi felt himself caught in the sucking grip of a whirlpool. He began to sink, fought his way back to the surface, and struck out desperately toward the nearby corvette, where already he could see shipmates being lifted to safety over a rope-ladder. Franzini was there, going up — and Brunetti — Giorgini — .

With his last bit of strength, Toschi reached the side of the corvette and grabbed the dangling ladder. He hung there a moment, swaying, then lifted his head. His eyes met the wry glance of a British seamen, looking down at him from the rail above. The seaman's face broke into a grin.

"Welcome aboard, mate. And congratulations. For you, the war is over."

As Toschi went up the ladder, the gunfire ceased. The sea went silent. The three British ships turned and moved off in column toward Alexandria Harbor, with the corvette and its cargo of downcast prisoners bringing up the rear.

And at that moment, some 2000 miles to the west, the *Scire* too was moving across a quiet sea, on her way back to La Spezia. There had been no attack at Gibraltar. Her radio instructions the night before had read: "British fleet units have left harbor. Return to home base." It had all been for nothing.

A strange coincidence, Borghese thought, as he studied the horizon from the conning tower bridge. Had the British been warned? After a time he shrugged the point aside; his business was to run the submarine.

Antonio Marceglia (left) and Spartaco Schergat, frogmen who knocked out *HMS Queen Elizabeth*.

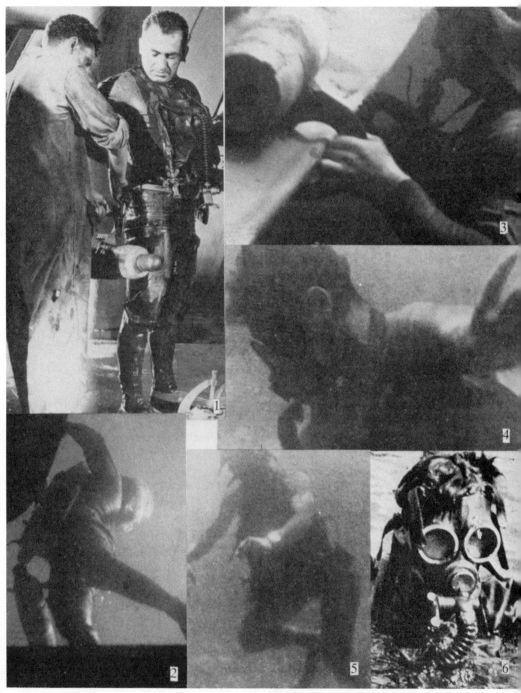

(1) Frogman aboard submarine dons assault gear; (2) makes underwater approach to hull of target ship; (3) fastens time bomb to bilge keel of ship; (4-6) leaves ship to swim away and wade ashore.

Chapter 9.
Return to the Rock

A s the *Scire* neared home, the big British warships returned to Gibraltar. One by one they moved in through the Straits, arriving back as quietly as they had departed, dropping anchor below La Linea in the Bay of Algeciras. Their return was duly noted and photographed by an Italian reconnaissance plane, and the news relayed to La Spezia.

Thus, four weeks later, the rising of October's moon found Borghese once again approaching the entrance of the Straits, guiding the *Scire* underwater by day and moving warily along on the surface by night. Aboard were the same human-torpedo teams that had accompanied him on the September mission — Tesei with Petty Officer Alcide Pedretti, Birindelli with Damos Paccagnini, de la Penne with Emilio Bianchi, and one crew in reserve. Unknown to either side, this was to be the start of a three-year war between the Tenth Light Flotilla and the Gibraltar defenses — a silent, underwater struggle in which the Serchio men were to sink or disable 14 Allied ships at a cost of only three men killed and three captured.

The *Scire* arrived at the Straits on October 27. That night, and again on the 28th, Borghese tried to penetrate the entrance, but the odds were too heavily against him; there were too many British destroyers and corvettes on the prowl. Finally, on the 29th, he risked a daytime underwater approach and succeeded; shortly after noon that day, the *Scire* lay submerged inside the entrance of the bay, 230 feet down, resting on the rocky bottom of the Spanish coast, waiting for darkness and for a chance to surface and proceed with her mission.

That evening, Borghese called the team leaders to a conference in the *Scire*'s small wardroom. The submarine was silent, except for an occasional hollow booming sound as eddying currents pushed the hull against sea-worn rocks. He poured wine, and the men took their seats around him.

"Tesei — de la Penne — Birindelli — your health," he said.

"Good health...long life." They drank.

"The big ships are at anchor in the harbor," he said. "Rome confirms it by radio. Two battleships, identified as such — cruisers — perhaps an aircraft carrier."

Tesei smiled. "It is good. So is the wine."

"Help yourself," said Borghese. "Now, this will be the target assignment. The battleship nearest the channel is the Barham."

He pointed it out on a broad chart that stretched across the wardroom table. "Birindelli, she's all yours; take her. Tesei, there's another battleship further away, right there near the North Mole. She's unidentified by name, but we think she may be the Warspite. In any event, she's yours. De la Penne, your job is to see if you can single out an aircraft carrier or heavy cruiser and take care of it. Use your own judgement. There are plenty of targets to choose from.

"Meanwhile, here's what we must do to get into position. To some extent, we'll have to run blind — because there's never been an Italian submarine in this bay before, either in wartime or peace. We are the first. So our sea-bed charts are crude. We could run into trouble.

"Nevertheless, here's our problem. We must decide at which point in the harbor to make the drop — where is the best point for you and your men to leave the Scire and mount your torpedoes — the takeoff point providing the best chance for success and escape. That brings up several difficult requirements.

"First, we need to be as close as possible to the harbor anchorage; that way, you won't have to waste time or risk exhaustion on a long approach. Second, we need a depth of at least 50 feet to let you get your torpedoes out of their cylinders underwater; any shallower and we'll invite detection. Third, we need to be reasonably distant from the area of normal patrol boat activity. Fourth, we must avoid any point where the currents may work against you. Any comments so far? Any suggestions?"

De la Penne grinned. "The British know all about this harbor. Why don't we send a man up and ask for directions?"

Borghese nodded in mock approval. "Very good, Luigi. That's your assignment in case we get stuck."

"I withdraw the proposal," said de la Penne.

Borghese bent over the table chart again. "Fortunately for Luigi and all the rest of us," he said, "there's one place that meets all our needs. Here, take a look." He stabbed the chart with a pencil point. "Right there — at the very mouth of the River Guadarranque."

The men studied the chart closely, murmuring approval. The spot was close to ideal. The water depth was just right. Where the Guadarranque flowed down from Spain and emptied into the bay, there would be a steady current working in their favor. It would be pushing them in a southeasterly direction, straight toward the enemy's anchorage. Their targets would be silhouetted against the lights of Gibraltar. Each team would be reasonably close to an escape route by way of the La Linea shore. And most of the British patrol craft activities probably would be concentrated at the farther end of the bay, to guard against intrusion from the Straits.

"We'll move to that position right now," Borghese decided. "It's not far away." As he spoke, the sound of twin propellers passed above them and faded in the distance. "That's the third one in twenty minutes," he remarked. "The sooner we get out of here, the better."

Tesei swallowed the last of his wine. "One question," he said.

"Yes, Teseo?"

"Our rendezvous with the escape agent. Any change in the arrangements?"

Borghese shook his head. "No change. The agent known as 'N' will be on the La Linea beach road at 8 o'clock tomorrow morning. When you get ashore and meet him, he'll take you around to Algeciras — to the Principe Alfonso Hotel — and you'll be safely at rest in Spain. Then you'll fly home."

The meeting came to an end. The torpedo-men shuffled to their feet and made their way to their bunks, to nap if possible and to store up energy for the hard hours ahead. Borghese went to the control room, to get the submarine under way and move to the departure point off the mouth of the Guadarranque. Again he heard the faint sound of propellers passing overhead, but he felt no concern. Things were going well.

And they were still going well at 2 o'clock the next morning, when the *Scire* rose from the harbor floor and quietly broke the dark surface of the bay. Moored alongside and surfacing with her came the three two-man torpedoes, already freed from their bulky steel cylinders during the time the submarine had been resting on the bottom.

The six torpedo-men, clad in their black underwater diving suits, followed Borghese through the conning tower hatch and down the bridge ladder to the deck below. They stared around at the outline of the harbor, getting their eyes adjusted to the night. They were in the dark, northern curve of the bay. To the southwest, street lights and moving automobile headlamps illuminated the shore of Algeciras. At the far southeast, the lights of Gibraltar flickered down across the North Mole, the South Mole, the Coal Pier, and an indistinct column of moored warships. Eastward, against the waterfront lights of La Linea, merchant ships were assembling for convoy. And moving here and there across the bay were the shadows of British patrol craft.

De la Penne shook his head in disapproval. "Careless, careless. You'd think they'd turn out those lights on Gibraltar."

"Just be grateful," said Borghese. He gathered the men around him, giving each one a farewell handshake. "All set?" he asked. "Everything in order?"

Tesei stepped forward. "Except for one thing," he said.

"One thing?" Borghese frowned. "What's that?"

"A simple request, Commander — that you give each of us a kick in the rear for good luck. Then we're on our way."

Borghese bowed. "Request granted, gentlemen. Remember, you asked for it."

One by one, he put them through the ritual, booting each man from behind as the six operators slipped overside to mount their waiting torpedoes. Then, with a wave of the hand, he went back inside the submarine, closed the hatch, and returned to the control room.

"Take her down," he ordered quietly. And a few minutes later, listening on the underwater hydrophones, he heard the sound of the two-man torpedoes in motion, fading away toward their targets. He glanced at his watch. It was 2:30 in the morning, time for the submarine to leave.

"Course one-nine-oh," he said to his helmsman.

"One-nine-oh, aye...Steady on one-nine-oh, sir."

The *Scire* moved out slowly, hugging the bottom, nosing down the bay to enter the Straits submerged and to set a homeward course for La Spezia. Her part of the mission was ended, carried out without a flaw.

HMS York, frogman target at Suda Bay.

British warships at Gibraltar anchorage.

Chapter 10.
Inside Gibraltar

For the submariners aboard the *Scire*, departure from Gibraltar meant the satisfying fulfillment of a demanding task.

For the men who were left behind though, for the torpedo-men, the trials for the night were just beginning — trials that rose swiftly from hardship to heartache. It was a night when the men strained and struggled to do their best, but when it so happened that their weapons and gear were plagued with one mechanical breakdown after another.

De la Penne and Bianchi had scarcely left the side of the *Scire* before their compass jammed. They shrugged this off as being relatively unimportant since the town of Gibraltar was plainly visible ahead of them, glimmering with lights and clearly outlined against the darkness of the towering rock; that would be their guide.

They set out on a direct course, then, with only their heads showing above water, moving smoothly toward the harbor anchorage. But just 20 minutes later, as they slipped along through the dark water, a cruising patrol boat caught the sound of their approach on its detectors. For an instant, four brilliant searchlight beams stabbed through the darkness and caught their wake in a full glare of light. They submerged quickly, leveling off at 50 feet and going ahead without breaking speed. Above them, the lights snapped off.

For 10 more minutes, de la Penne kept to their course without slackening. Then, the impact of an underwater explosion jarred their torpedo. Its motor coughed, sputtered and died. They began to sink, dropping further and further down despite their frantic efforts to level off. Finally they touched bottom at 130 feet; and at that point the torpedo stubbornly refused to move. No amount of effort could get the motor or the exhaust pumps working again. The vehicle lay canted on its side, as lifeless as a sunken hulk.

For close to an hour, the two torpedo-men wrestled with their disabled craft, trying in vain to restore it to buoyancy, gradually growing weaker as their air supply thinned out and as the icy chill of the water penetrated to their skin. Finally, exhausted by their efforts, de la Penne and Bianchi gave up the underwater struggle.

They swam to the surface, sank their breathing-gear equipment, and slowly began swimming in a direction away from Gibraltar, heading for a coastal point some two miles distant, carefully eluding patrol boats that at times passed them within 90 feet.

Close to two hours later, at 5:30 in the morning, they staggered ashore on a beach one mile north of Algeciras. There they shed their diving gear and began a wary walk along the La Linea road, looking for their escape agent. The man called 'N' was waiting for them, as promised, meeting them on the highway at 7:30. He hid them in the back of his car, while he went in search of the other teams.

"A miserable failure," said Bianchi, as they curled down out of sight of passing traffic. "Not a single ship to our credit."

De la Penne patted his shoulder. "At least we're still alive. There'll be other chances. Anyhow, blame the equipment and not yourself. Nobody can do much with a piece of dead metal."

Meanwhile Tesei and Pedretti had also been plagued by problems. No sooner had they mounted their torpedo, alongside the *Scire*, than they discovered that the weapon's instrument panel was clouded beyond reading, their compass was performing erratically, and the torpedo's trimming gear was partially jammed. Regardless, they got under way and maneuvered easterly to a point some 500 yards from the shoreline, within sound of breaking surf. The night was quiet, but patrol boats were cruising nearby and the strong phosphorescence in the water was giving the torpedo a bright wake. To play safe, the men set a dead-reckoning course for the lights of Gibraltar and then submerged to 50 feet, to make their approach underwater.

At about 5 o'clock in the morning, they surfaced to get their bearings. Their navigation had been flawless. They were close to the North Mole, behind which loomed their battleship target, moored near the northern entrance of the anchorage.

Tesei quickly began making preparations to submerge again and to begin the approach for attack. But at this point, both sets of breathing-gear gave out within moments of each other. Tesei kept the torpedo circling slowly while he pulled the reserve breathing-gear from its container. That too proved useless, jammed and kinked because of faulty stowage. And suddenly, reacting to the malfunction of its trimming pump, the torpedo itself dipped sharply at the stern and hung awkwardly in that angular position.

Tesei swore under his breath. Without the breathing-gear, they could not possibly reach the battleship underwater. To proceed on the surface would be to invite certain failure and probably raise an alarm that would jeopardize the other two teams. There was nothing to do, then, but to give up the attack and withdraw.

As quietly as possible, the two men detached the torpedo's warhead and let it sink to the bottom. Then they turned toward the lights of La Linea and slowly moved off in the direction of the shore. They landed on the beach shortly after 7 o'clock, buried their breathing-gear, opened the flooding tank of the torpedo, and sent the weapon back into the bay, watching it cruise off toward the south. Then they set out along the beach road for their rendezvous with 'N'. They found him within the hour, and joined their shipmates de la Penne and Bianchi in the getaway car.

"We'll wait for your two other friends until 8:30," 'N' told them, "If they're not here by that time, my orders are to take you directly to Algeciras."

"Fair enough," said de la Penne. "We all know the risks."

Meanwhile the team of Birindelli and Paccagnini also had moved off to a bad start. As soon as they left the *Scire*, their trimming pump failed. Moments later, Paccagnini's breathing-gear developed a leak and he had to replace it with reserve equipment. Next, their torpedo began to wallow heavily and to lose speed, partly because of the trimming pump failure and partly because of sea water leaking into the batteries.

Nevertheless, with only their heads showing above water, they set out on a course toward Gibraltar's lights. By 4 o'clock in the morning they were nearing the anchorage, occasionally passing so close between rows of British ships that they could hear the conversation of lookouts on deck. For more than two hours, they moved warily along on their course toward the anchorage entrance until, shortly before 7 o'clock, they arrived at a double barrier composed of huge floats, moored 20 feet apart and connected by spiked iron bars.

They paused briefly, sizing up the situation and listening to the voices of sentries on the pier overhead. Then, ever so cautiously, they threaded their torpedo through the two lines of barriers and emerged, still surfaced, on the far side.

The dim silhouettes of big ships lay just ahead. Birindelli studied them closely, then raised his hand to draw his partner's attention. There, less than 300 yards away, was the battleship *Barham*. They were directly on its beam. They reacted quickly, submerging with their torpedo until they touched bottom at 45 feet. It was time to prepare to attack.

But once again, at a crucial moment in the operation, trouble arose. Paccagnini's supply of oxygen gave out without warning, leaving him no choice but to swim to the surface and try to escape by himself.

Birindelli, working alone on the rock-strewn bottom, quickly managed to get the human-torpedo under way and headed toward the *Barham*. But again came trouble. He had traveled for 10 minutes through the darkness, making slow progress and frequently bumping against sharp outcroppings on the harbor floor, but moving ever closer to his target. Then, for no apparent reason, the torpedo abruptly stopped its forward motion and sank to the bottom. He checked for the trouble, but could not find it. The situation had him completely baffled. The propeller was clear, the motor was responding smoothly; and yet the craft refused to move.

Finally Birindelli decided to pull the torpedo to the ship by sheer muscle rather than abandon his mission. Accordingly, to make sure of his location, he looped a guideline to the weapon and then swam to the surface, looking around warily with only the top of his head above water. As his eyes adjusted, he saw that the *Barham* was close by, looming against the night, just over 200 feet away. He grunted with satisfaction; an easy target. He ducked under again and swam back to the bottom. There he slung another loop around the torpedo, tested it for tension, and began to pull.

It was painful, agonizing work. And it was futile. After 30 minutes of wrenching strain, he found he had moved the torpedo forward by only a few feet at best; and, alarmingly, he was beginning to feel the symptoms of an approaching blackout. Obviously, the task was impossible.

He rested a moment until his mind cleared. He contemplated his defeat with bitterness — to be so close to success, and yet to fail. "At least," he told himself, "I can leave them my calling card." Encouraged by that thought, he activated the time-fuse on the torpedo's warhead and then swam back to the surface, hoping by now only to get back into the open bay and swim to the Spanish coast before being discovered by British patrols.

Then began an ordeal of suspense and effort. Birindelli got past the iron spikes of the first obstruction barrier and rested at the second, clinging to a shadowed buoy. There he got rid of his breathing-gear and his diving suit, lashing them together in a heavy package. They sank to the bottom, leaving him dressed in his Navy fatigues. He slipped into the water again and swam along for some 200 yards, hugging the dark, protective coverage of the Coal Pier. Suddenly, sharp cramps gripped his belly, doubling him over, stabbing in painful waves that made him long to cry out. He looked around frantically for a means of relief, found a dangling steel cable, and pulled himself up to the exposed surface of the pier. There he lay unmoving for some 20 minutes, gradually feeling the cramps go away and his strength return. He realized, resignedly, that any further swimming was out of the question; he would have to make his way on foot.

Moving once again, Birindelli slipped from the shadow of one coal pile to another and eventually reached the North Mole. Somehow, timing his movements and going from coverage to coverage, he got past the sentry post at the narrowest, most dangerous point of the mole and hid behind a pile of harbor nets on the other side. There he realized to his dismay that the darkness of night had weakened considerably, and the telltale grey of dawn was moving up the sky. Workmen and soldiers were beginning to straggle out along the mole, heading for their duty stations. Unless he moved quickly, he told himself, he would certainly be discovered. Accordingly, he rolled up his sleeves to hide his insignia of rank and boldly stepped out on the walkway of the mole, striding briskly off in the direction of the mainland, mingling with the workers who were going off duty. Several men, passing by, stared curiously at his water-soaked clothing; but nobody attempted to stop him for questioning.

A short distance down the mole, Birindelli came abreast of a small Spanish ship, the *Santa Anna*, moored outboard to the pier. This, he decided, could be his refuge. He glanced about in the spreading daylight, saw nobody paying any attention to him, and then stepped aboard to look for a hiding place.

But at that point, he was brought up short. A British Commander and two Gibraltar policemen, coming down the mole, spotted him and stepped aboard directly behind him.

"Your identification, please," the Commander demanded.

Birindelli shrugged. He had played his luck as far as it would go. He reached into his wet clothing and produced his Navy I.D.card.

"So that's it! An Italian spy!"

"Quite wrong," said Birindelli. "An Italian officer." He rolled down his sleeves, displaying his rank.

And at that precise moment, out in the anchorage, the torpedo warhead exploded. A roaring boom hurled its echoes against Gibraltar's rock and shook the piers. A towering geyser of dirty gray water shot high into the air, spraying the decks of nearby ships. Immediately sirens began whooping, destroyers went foaming out across the water, the harbor became a turmoil of noise and action.

Birindelli took in the scene and began to chuckle. The Commander stared at him curiously, gave him a nod of appraisal, and handed back the card. "If you're who I think you are, you're late," he said. "Your friends were hanging around La Linea beach for a while, but by now they're safely at their hotel in Algeciras. Oh, and we captured your partner too — caught him swimming around in the middle of the bay. So come along, now. Let's go to prison."

Birindelli went along quietly, with confidence. He already knew how to get his coded report back to Serchio through censored mail. His shipmates would soon learn the details of his experience, and would be better prepared for their next mission. That was all that mattered at the moment.

On the next day, in the Spanish newspaper *Informaciones*, there appeared a short news item which read:

ITALIAN SUBMARINE NEAR GIBRALTAR?

La Linea, 31st October — Persistent rumors among the inhabitants here assert that on the morning of the 30th an Italian submarine succeeded in approaching at night the entrance to the harbor of Gibraltar and in firing a torpedo which damaged the anti-submarine net guarding the harbor.

This bit of information dove-tailed with an official release put out the same day by the British Naval Command at Gibraltar, which read:

"An unsuccessful attempt was made this morning by officers of the Italian Navy to blow up vessels in harbor by means of a special contrivance. One charge exploded, without doing any damage, in the entrance to the harbor and another was stranded on a beach in Spanish territory."

The stranded weapon was Tesei's unmanned torpedo, which he had sent off to lose itself on the floor of the bay. Instead, however, it had veered sharply to the east, for some unknown reason, and had wound up ashore, where Spanish technicians had seized it for dismantling and examination.

That development was reported on November 2, in the *A. B. C.* journal of Madrid:

Algeciras, 1st November — The apparatus found on Espigon Beach at La Linea passed through this city on its way to San Fernando for examination at the La Carraca works. The contrivance is 5 meters long and is shaped like an ordinary torpedo, but new features are a couple of small seats of identical form and some hand-levers. Nothing is known about the crew, but it is supposed that the apparatus, like that which exploded against the defense net of the harbor of Gibraltar, must have been launched by some secret process from a submarine, a ship or an aircraft. When it was found on the beach at La Linea, the propeller was still in motion.

So, then, the secret was out. To the men at River Serchio, however, the mission was nevertheless a success from several points of view. First, it had provided valuable experience for the crews of the Tenth Light Flotilla. Second, the *Scire* had proved the principle of submarine assault-transportation to be sound. Third, weak points and flaws in the weapons and gear had been discovered and could be easily rectified. Fourth, it had demonstrated that the torpedo-men could do their job efficiently and effectively, provided they were given good material to work with. And fifth, the crews of the enemy ships henceforth would feel uneasy even when moored in protected harbors.

And meanwhile in Rome, all details of the operation quickly came to rest on the desk of Benito Mussolini.

The Duce immediately sent for Prince Borghese, summoning him to Palazzo Venezia to give a personal account of the operation. The two had met a few years earlier, at a Navy luncheon held at the Armed Forces Club in Rome. Then, the atmosphere had been cheerful and bright, with Mussolini boasting of his successes in Ethiopia and in the Spanish Civil War. This time, the atmosphere was grim; the Duce had just been informed of the bad news from the Albanian Front, where the war against Greece was going so badly that it appeared he might soon have to undergo the humiliation of asking Hitler to send help.

When he received Borghese, he was wearing striped trousers and a black jacket instead of his usual bemedalled uniform. He stood behind his huge desk, looking worn and weary. But he stared with sharp interest at the charts and forms that Borghese had brought along to illustrate his report; and, more than any other point, he seemed fascinated by the fact that Gibraltar's lights were still burning nightly, as though the British on the base refused to take the war seriously.

Borghese gave his full report, picked up his charts and papers, and stood at attention, waiting for further orders.

Mussolini was silent for several moments, as though pondering the details he had just heard. Finally he spoke.

"You have my congratulations," he said. "Continue your work — persevere in the name of all Italians.

"You may now withdraw."

Chapter 11.
Victory at Suda Bay

L ate one November night in 1940, Commander Vittorio Mocca-gatta sat at the small desk in his bedroom at River Serchio and finished writing the day's entry in his war diary.

"I am now giving the whole of my time to organizing the special weapons division," he wrote. "I have stopped all reading and the spending of any time on my own account, but I am more than glad to do so. I shall have to keep a cool head for the future in order to obtain positive results. However, I have two excellent men in support of me to carry out my programs — Lieutenant Commander Valerio Borghese in charge of the underwater assault teams, and Lieutenant Commander Giorgio Giobbe in charge of the surface teams. I count on them for strength and dedication."

With that, Moccagatta closed his diary for the night. He leaned back in his chair, noting that it was long past his bedtime. He sat on, however, sipping a glass of wine and enjoying the cool autumn air that drifted in through his bedroom window. Relaxing, he let his thoughts run over the situation that now confronted him.

As Commanding Officer of the Tenth Light Flotilla — the first permanent C.O. since Mario Giorgini had been captured by the British — he was now faced with the demanding task of advancing the special-weapons program over the final bumps and handicaps caused by faulty equipment, and of putting it into smooth operation as a dependable implement of warfare. He was confident he would succeed.

He had spent almost his entire career in the Navy serving aboard the big warships. He was totally familiar with the ways of cruisers and battleships and the like. But that was in the past; for the present, he was fascinated by the potential of the secret-weapons program and was willing to stake his professional future on its success. He was a strict disciplinarian, a tireless worker, and a talented organizer and administrator. He had attacked his new assignment with enthusiasm. The operation at Gibraltar had proved to him that the human-torpedo teams could successfully penetrate enemy harbors. Now he intended to prove that one-man explosive assault boats — the E-boats — could do the same. Then, putting the two together, the Navy would have a truly lethal secret-weapon force.

He nodded approval. The picture pleased him.

Just four months later came his opportunity to launch a full-scale E-boat attack against enemy warships. It happened at Suda Bay, on the northern coast of Crete.

By early 1941, Crete had become a critical pressure point for the Axis and Allied powers alike in their struggle to control the Mediterranean. Its location, directly south of the Peleponnesos Peninsula, gave it domain over the Dodecanese Islands and the southern sweep of the Aegean Sea. It lay athwart the British convoy lanes running between Greece and Alexandria. Similarly, it was a prime position from which to strike at the Axis supply lines running from Italy to Benghasi and Tobruk. Whoever controlled Crete, controlled a strategic key to the entire eastern Mediterranean. And whoever controlled Suda Bay, controlled Crete.

For many centuries, Suda Bay has been known to seafaring men as one of the world's great natural harbors. It is a narrow, sheltered, deep-water anchorage, so deep in fact that ships must go well inside to its farther western arc before they can anchor securely. There, six miles or more from the open sea, they are protected by a curving range of high, wild cliffs and rugged slopes, many of them bristling with gun emplacements trained on the waters below.

On paper at least, as Moccagatta admitted to himself, Suda Bay looked like nothing better than a death trap for any attackers trying to enter with explosive motorboats. Considering the guns in the hills, and the three lines of buoyed barriers in the bay itself, it would appear almost impossible to penetrate to the anchorage. And if penetration were by any chance successful, it would be utterly impossible for the assault-men to escape back to the open sea. Their choice would be simple: death or capture.

Nevertheless, in Moccagatta's opinion, the attack should be made. Photographs by air reconnaissance showed strong British naval units coming and going almost daily. Tankers and supply ships were regularly at anchor in the sheltered head of the bay. Destroyers came and went in steady numbers. Cruisers were frequently on hand — the *Coventry*, the *Gloucester*, the *Carlisle*, the heavy-gunned *York*. The value of destroying any one of these targets was too much to ignore: and to destroy the *York* particularly would be to inflict heavy damage against Britain's Mediterranean power, both physically and psychologically.

Thus, in late January, Moccagatta flew to an Italian advanced base on the island of Leros and called a conference of selected E-boat operators. They met in the wardroom of the destroyer *Crispi*, at tables covered with charts and maps and aerial photos of British shipping and Suda Bay defenses. They talked for hours, planning target assignments and details of attack.

Finally Moccagatta brought the meeting to a close.

"Gentlemen," he said, "you are not to rush this attack. You must wait until everything is right for success — a favorable moon, calm seas, easy wind, and of course the necessary targets at anchor. Wait for weeks if you have to — but make it right. There will be no excuse for failure. I am taking the word of Lieutenant Commander Giobbe that you six are the best E-boat men in the Navy. This is your chance to prove him correct.

"Lieutenant Luigi Faggioni, here, will command the operation. He and Alessio De Vito and Emilio Barberi will sail with this ship, the Crispi. We have also been allotted the destroyer Sella. She will transport the other three men — Angelo Cabrini, Tullio Tedeschi and Lino Beccati. Six assault boats in all.

"When the time and the conditions are right, you will sail from Stampalia near the Cretan coast, with three E-boats aboard each ship. You will be dropped ten miles from the entrance to Suda Bay. And Faggioni will take over from there.

"Now for your final requirement. Regardless of risk or cost, you are to destroy the cruiser York. Are there any question?"

"Yes," said Faggioni. "Why is the York our prime target? And incidentally, the British may be grateful. She's the ugliest ship in the whole Royal Navy."

Moccagatta nodded; Faggioni's appraisal was justified. In the eye of any good Navy man, the *York* was a grotesque looking ship. All through construction, her design and purpose had kept changing — from battle cruiser, to anti-aircraft cruiser, to scout cruiser with planes, and finally in 1928 to heavy cruiser with overweight guns. In the end, she emerged as an awkward looking vessel with misshapen stacks and malformed rigging, but nevertheless a warship of tremendous fire-power.

"I agree," he told Faggioni. "When they built her, they couldn't make up their minds what they were doing. But regardless, we want her put out of action permanently. Not because she's ugly, but for a very critical reason: she has the biggest, most deadly cruiser guns in the Mediterranean — and perhaps in the world. See that they're silenced. You can believe me, the British won't thank us for that. So now," he said rising, "this meeting is over. I leave you on your own."

On the night of March 25, all elements favorable for the attack fell into place. The sky was dark and overcast. The sea was calm. The wind was light and blowing gently from the southwest. And a dispatch from air reconnaissance reported that, at the far end of Suda Bay, riding quietly at anchor, were three British oil tankers, two staff ships, eight cargo ships, two destroyers, and the heavy cruisers *Coventry*, *Gloucester* and *York*. Faggioni called his men together. It was time for the E-boats to make their move.

Speeding out from Stampalia, the *Crispi* and the *Sella* reached the assigned departure point northeast of Suda's entrance at 11:31 that night and lowered the six boats into the water less than a minute later. The destroyers then turned away, as the E-boats moved out in a rhomboid formation with Faggioni and Cabrini in the lead. Three hours later, the assault-men reached the first of the harbor's barriers, a buoyed line of defenses that stretched across the bay's entrance and were anchored, near mid-stream, to the hulking rocky base of old Fort Suda.

It took only a few minutes for Faggioni to lead the way over the barrier, slipping between two buoys near the center of the entrance. In another 15 minutes he had reached and crossed the second barrier, this time choosing a point farther to the right where he could take advantage of the shadows cast by sea-washed rocks. Behind him, one by one, the other five boats slipped across the barrier and fell into column. It was 2:45 in the morning.

Faggioni swung his attack force to the left, curving out to the middle of the dark bay, and then began traveling the long leg toward the distant anchorage barrier. He had gauged his speed to achieve arrival in approximately two hours, allowing a small margin of time before dawn.

Only one incident interrupted their journey. That took place just briefly, when they had covered slightly more than half the distance to their goal. At that point, from a hilltop on their left, two searchlights suddenly flashed on, sweeping their cones of light back and forth across the water directly ahead. Faggioni throttled his engine and signaled the column to a halt. For several minutes they waited in tense silence, their boats drifting idly as wavelets lapped against them in the darkness. The two beams sent shining pools of light sliding across the stretch of bay ahead. For an instant, one angled off to the far right and illuminated a gap in the anchorage barrier.

"Thank you," Faggioni murmured. "I was wondering about that."

The the lights snapped off and the bay went dark again. The E-boats moved ahead once more, this time on a slanting course toward where the barrier gap had come into view.

It was 4:30 by Faggioni's luminous watch when the E-boats arrived at the barrier and assembled to make their way through. The route that lay open was a gap about 50 yards wide, lying between the end of the buoy line and the rocky shore at the northern extreme of the barrier. As they slipped by, concealed by the shadow of the rocks, the assault-men could plainly hear the voices of the British sentries on shore and the barking of a dog in the distance.

The boats turned in line behind Faggioni, glided through the barrier and angled left, running parallel to the net until they reached the middle of the bay. There they grouped around Faggioni and shut off their motors, clinging to each other's boats in the darkness. Nearby they could see the dim, blurred outlines of big ships at anchor. It was 4:46, not quite time yet to synchronize their attack with early light.

Faggioni left his men in their group, turned his boat, and moved off by himself to identify ships and targets. Directly ahead of him was the cruiser *York*, easily recognizable by her grotesque stacks. She lay broadside to the barrier with her starboard beam exposed to the attack route. He looked around for other cruisers, but saw none. Perhaps they had moved out during early evening.

Just beyond the *York*, though, and to the right, he identified two large ships as cargo vessels. He wondered if they might be carrying munitions. Closer to hand, and off to the left, lay a huge oil tanker, the *Pericles*, riding low in the water with a full cargo of fuel. Faggioni noted the ships' positions, and quietly returned to his E-boat group.

He drew the others around him, and held out the lone pair of night binoculars in his equipment. They were passed from hand to hand, so that each man might study his target as Faggioni gave out the assignments.

When he spoke, he kept his voice low and hushed. "Cabrini and Tedeschi — your target is the York. She's the ship directly out ahead. Her ventilator fans are making a loud noise, and the sound will cover your approach. Move to within 200 yards of her and wait for my signal.

"You, De Vito — your assignment is a cargo ship, just beyond the York and to the right. There are two of them there. Take your choice. You, Barberi — that big hulking shadow off to the left is a loaded tanker, the Pericles. That's your target. She'll make a glorious fire.

"Meanwhile, Beccati and I will hold back to see how things develop. Then we'll pick a target and attack."

He paused. "We'll be getting first light in about ten minutes — just before 5:30. That's when I'll give the signal to hit the York. The rest of you, move out at the same time. Any question?"

Whispers came, "None, Luigi...All set."

"Good." Faggioni leaned forward and handed each man a small bottle of cognac. They drank quickly, toasting each other in silence and letting the empty bottles slide into the water.

"Now then, get into position," he told them. "Go with my signal. And God be with you all."

Minutes later, aboard the *York*, Lieutenant Robin Buckley took a break from his monotonous pacing back and forth on the bridge to check the ship's security and operational readiness. As Torpedo Officer, he was in charge of the duty watch. It had been a quiet night , with the harbor cloaked in deep blackness by the shadows of the cliffs that rimmed the bay. In low-voiced tones, activating his sound-telephone circuit, he called for routine reports. They were normal; all standby gun crews were on station. Below decks, engine room and boiler room personnel were at work building steam in the ship's tubes. Cooks and stewards were busy in the galley, preparing sausages for breakfast. The skipper, Captain Reginald Portal was asleep in his quarters, but would have to be called within a few more minutes. The Executive Officer, Commander Cowley Thomas, probably would come to the bridge in a moment or two. The Navigation Officer, Lieutenant David Tibbits, was getting out of bed at that very moment, or should be.

Buckley walked to the port wing of the bridge, leaned on the coaming, and stared into the darkness astern. Back there, some 300 yards off the quarter, the cruiser *Coventry* was preparing to leave the port side of the tanker *Pericles*, where she had been moored for the past four hours while taking on fuel. Buckley rubbed his cheeks, satisfied with his brief survey. All was normal for the start of what he supposed would be a busy day at sea.

He ran his mind through the posted orders for the ship's routine:

26 March

0515 — Reveille.

0545 — Action stations, prepare

for leaving harbor.

0600 — Weigh anchor and proceed.

A sudden, distant sound caused him to tilt his head. He cupped an ear and muttered to himself impatiently, irritated by the constant overpowering roar of the ship's ventilators. Above the loud din of the fans, from somewhere off to starboard, he could hear the rising noise of live engines racing across the water, drawing near. Well, that was normal enough, he decided; probably the usual British seaplanes, warming up to take off and fly out on dawn patrol. The sky was beginning to pale. Another few minutes, he reflected, and he'd be able to see what was going on around him instead of having to deal with sounds in the darkness. The noise of racing engines grew closer. He glanced at the luminous dial of his watch. It was 5:15.

Precisely on time, the notes of the bugle sounding reveille rang out aboard ship.

And seconds later, with a roaring scream of engines, there came a tremendous two-hit explosion against the hull of the *York*. The big ship whipped like an angry shark, then took a sickening lurch to starboard. "Air raid!" came a frantic shout.

In the welter of chaos that followed, alarms clattered, men rushed to battle stations, anti-aircraft guns ripped the sky with tracers, shells blasted overhead, machine guns poured a rain of fire into the clouds, emergency orders barked and echoed throughout the stricken ship.

Abruptly, another explosion nearby tore a great gash in the stern of the *Pericles*. Flames erupted, and a river of oil began to gush into the harbor. Then a third explosion, and a cargo ship heeled over, rocked back, and began to sink. Then another.

Aboard the *York*, Captain Portal rushed to the bridge and fought desperately to save his ship. She had been hit squarely amidships, at the bulkhead between the after boiler room and the forward engine room. A torrent of sea water flooded the two huge compartments almost instantly, leaving the ship without steam or power. Within moments, the *York* was going down by the stern, threatening to plunge to the bottom.

A Greek salvage tug and the British destroyer *Hasty* rushed forward foaming to the cruiser's side and heaved tow lines aboard. Portal ordered his deck crew to slip the anchor cable.

"Get us to the shallows if you can!" he shouted to the *Hasty*. "There's 140 feet of water under us!"

Slowly, limpingly, the *York* was pulled toward the beach. At last she grounded her stern. Her quarterdeck was awash, all her after compartments were flooded, and her hull was ripped open in a monstrous, gaping hole; she was finished.

Meanwhile from the instant of the attack, Faggioni had waited in his E-boat at the takeoff point, checking developments. He had heard Barberi's boat falter, hung up on a mooring buoy line. He had released Beccati in Barberi's place, rushing him out to hit the *Pericles*. Now Faggioni caught sight of a massive shadow emerging into view from beyond the hidden side of the tanker. He stared for moment, then kicked his boat into action with a surge of speed. The moving shadow was a cruiser, gaining headway and gliding out of the harbor. He drew aim on it at a widening angle, locked his rudder, pushed the throttle wide open and flung himself into the sea. Seconds later, his explosive boat passed directly astern of the *Coventry*, missing the big ship by a scant four feet.

Within the next three hours, all six of the E-boat men were hunted down by the British, captured and manacled.

Faggioni, swimming toward the beach, was in the water only 20 minutes when he was spotted by a four-man patrol boat crew and plucked from the harbor. His rescuers propped him up in the middle of their boat and stared at him. They were still convinced there had been an air raid.

"He'd be the pilot," said one of them. "At least we've shot down the God damned airplane. That's some satisfaction."

Faggioni smiled to himself and said nothing.

"Care for a cigarette?" they offered. "A nip of good whiskey?"

"Thanks," he said. "You're very kind."

"Why not? You're out of the war now. Your pals too, when we get them."

Cabrini had spent an hour in the water before two men in a lifeboat found him and took him aboard. He lay at their feet, exhausted and shivering, while one of his captors covered him with a cocked pistol. Then, "Put the gun away, mate," said the other at last. "He'll be no trouble. Let's just give him a cigarette and take him ashore."

Tedeschi was discovered and captured after two hours in the water. So were Beccati and Barberi. De Vito managed to get ashore on a harbor island, where he was captured almost at once by Greek soldiers.

By mid-morning, all six of the men had been rounded up and escorted by armed guards to a British military lockup at Castle Paleo-castro on the south shore of the bay. Long, tedious months of imprisonment lay ahead of them, they knew. But they were in good spirits. Behind them, in the oil-coated waters of the harbor, lay the wreckage of a cruiser, two large tankers and a cargo ship. A splendid victory for River Serchio.

Within a month, details of the attack were reported back to La Spezia through coded messages sent home by the prisoners in letters to their families. Commander Moccagatta read the accounts with pride and entered them in his war diary. Then he added a note of his own:

"One could really go to the end of the world with people like this."

Chapter 12.
Eyes on Malta

On the eve of Italy's entry into World War II, Mussolini had sent for his Chief of Staff, Marshal Badoglio, and asked him, "What plans do you have for Malta?"

Badoglio seemed quite surprised. "Malta? We don't have any," he said.

This was almost too much for Mussolini to believe. For 35 centuries, the island of Malta had been a central key to control of the Mediterranean. It had served that purpose under the successive rule of Phoenicians, Carthaginians, Romans, Arabs, Normans, Crusaders, French and British. It lay less than 60 miles from Sicily and 180 from Africa, standing astride the great east-west sea lanes between Gibraltar and Alexandria. Intricate networks of defense, built upon massive rocky cliffs by generations of warriors, protected its Grand Harbor and its capital city of Valletta. It was small in size, embracing only 96 square miles of territory. But it was a giant of strength, from the military strategist's point of view.

Thus, from a shocked Mussolini in 1940, "No plan at all for Malta?" Badoglio shrugged. "Nothing at all. Not that I'm aware of."

By the spring of 1941, however, a plan for Malta had taken shape, if only in the fantasies of Vittorio Moccagatta and Teseo Tesei.

The E-boat victory at Suda Bay had fired the imaginations of both men into planning for a quick, follow-up blow. They agreed that this should be at Malta, a night attack against Valletta and Grand Harbor, with a combined force of assault boats and human-torpedoes. Barely a month after Suda, therefore, they were spending their evenings at River Serchio plotting how best and when to hit the island fortress.

Borghese was vehemently opposed to the idea. So was his Serchio counterpart, Giorgio Giobbe. They made it their business to sit late at night with Moccagatta and Tesei, denouncing the Malta plan with outspoken bluntness, pounding away at its weak points and its lack of common sense.

"But it's insane!" Borghese stormed. "To begin with, there aren't any worthwhile targets there. You're asking a lot of men to kill themselves for nothing. And do you think for one moment that Rome will support you? I have it on the word of Count Galeazzo Ciano that Italy has no intention of attacking Malta. That information comes straight from Mussolini himself. Furthermore, do you realize we don't even have one solitary intelligence agent on the island? How can you plan an attack when you don't know what the enemy's doing? The whole thing is crazy!"

"I've already spoken to Admiral de Courten," Moccagatta replied crisply. "I have his full support. He likes the idea. He has told me to go ahead and work it out with Rome. I intend to do so. And what's more, I don't think the Admiral would be pleased with your reaction."

Borghese shook his head grimly. "No! — and for all I care, you can tell de Courten how I feel. But with all due respect to the Admiral, and to you personally, you're both being swayed by your years of training with the fleet. You can't get out of the habit of thinking in terms of big ships and heavy guns. And that is wrong. Wrong, because you're not thinking the way an assault-team specialist is supposed to think.

"Look — our mission is not to engage in surface bombardments, not to storm fortifications. Our mission is to make lightning surprise attacks against critical enemy shipping. And there aren't enough such ships at Valletta to make a raid worthwhile."

"How do you know that?" said Moccagatta.

"The same way you do — or should," said Borghese. "You know as well as I do that when Italy entered the war, England moved her big ships out of Malta. She had to — or leave them like sitting targets for air raids from Sicily, only ten minutes away.

"So she dispersed her fleet — divided the ships between Alexandria and Gibraltar, safely out of striking range by air. That's where we ought to be concentrating, where the ships are."

"They still come and go at Valletta," Moccagatta protested. "Air reconnaissance says so, the photographs prove it."

"A photograph can be out of date by the time it is developed." Borghese scoffed. "True, you'll find an occasional battleship or aircraft carrier stopping off at Malta. But only briefly, and never with enough frequency or regularity to justify planning an attack. They can be there and gone in the time it would take us to sail across from Sicily. Even if I could get ten torpedo-men into Grand Harbor, and Giobbe could get ten E-boats in there, the odds are they wouldn't find the kind of targets they're trained to destroy. And most of them would get killed while looking around. I say forget the whole thing."

Moccagatta shook his head and turned to Giobbe. "And you, Giorgio? Surely you don't agree with Valerio's thinking?"

"I most certainly do," said Giobbe. "He's thinking exactly the way we're supposed to think. Furthermore, how do you propose to break through those harbor defenses at Malta? That's a job for a battle fleet with heavy air support. For a team like ours, those defenses are just about impregnable."

Moccagatta smiled caustically. "So was Suda Bay. Impossible to penetrate, remember? And where's the mighty York tonight?"

"No, no, no," said Giobbe. "There's a world of difference between the two harbors. Just look at the chart, here. Look at those powerful batteries on each side of the entrance. They'll pin us down before we even reach the barriers. Look at the bridge running out to St. Elmo Mole, at the bridge abutments. Look at the Mole itself, barring the entrance — and the guns on the cliffs of Valletta. It's not like slipping quietly into Suda Bay. It's more like sliding head first down the mouth of a cannon and waiting for it to go off. And as Valerio says — if you get inside, where are your critical targets? What do you attack? A few destroyers? Trawlers? Irrelevant ships? The war will go on without them. I agree with Valerio. My advice is to forget it."

"But no!" Tesei leaned forward and banged the table sharply. The others stared at him, startled by his outburst. "You two gentlemen are my dear friends," he said in sober tones. "But I must disagree with you utterly, and side with the Commander. You have missed the crucial point."

"Which is?" said Borghese.

"Which is this," said Tesei. "The whole world must be made to realize that we Italians are ready to attack Malta in the most daring way and regardless of the outcome. We must seize this chance to prove ourselves.

"Whether we sink any ships there or not does not matter. What does matter is that we prove able and willing to be blown up with our craft, under the very noses of the enemy. We will then have shown our sons and future generations of Italians at what sacrifice we follow our ideals, and at what price we reach for success!"

The room was silent for several long moments. Then Borghese spoke, in low tones. "Tesei," he said slowly. "Are you seriously advocating mass suicide?"

Tesei stared back at him. "I can only speak for myself, Valerio," he said. "A man must live or die by his own principles. I feel I have a sacred obligation to my country. I intend to honor it by giving my life."

In the long stillness that followed, Tesei's three companions studied him with looks of mingled compassion and respect. Then Moccagatta arose from his chair and spoke quietly. "It's time to end this meeting," he said. "Let's all get a good sleep. We'll talk more in the morning."

By morning, however, Moccagatta on impulse had gone off to Rome, to seek support for his Malta-attack plan from influential friends at Supermarina. To his dismay, he found them far from enthusiastic about his proposal. They made it clear that they liked and respected both Moccagatta and Admiral de Courten, that they held the career records of both men in high esteem, that they had been deeply impressed by the stunning victory at Suda Bay. But, to attack Malta? — were there any good targets there? — did anyone actually know what might be going on behind the defenses? — or what surprises the British might be hiding?

The result was that Moccagatta spent more than two weeks in Rome going from office to office, knocking on door after door, sharing drinks and cigars with one old friend after another — each of whom seemed delighted to see him, but relieved to pass him along to somebody else.

He began to feel increasingly discouraged, but still stubbornly determined to push for his plan.

On May 10, he wrote in his diary:

"Today the memorandum was drawn up about the operation against Malta. But this evening it seemed to me that the Deputy Chief of Staff, Admiral Campioni, is still dubious about the opportune value of the plan. We shall have to answer soon but it's heavy going."

By May 22, the "heavy going" seemed to be producing at least a grudging willingness to let Moccagatta dig up more facts in support of his plan:

"On the morning of the 20th (he wrote), I was received by the Under Secretary but he would not give me a free hand for the Malta operation. As I had suggested that, before embarking upon the operation itself, we should have a stab at the outer defenses with two motorboats, the Under Secretary told me to make two of these thrusts and then report to him about them. If I could conscientiously advise him that the operation was practicable, he said, he would consider giving an order to proceed. The crews are very keen and want to get into action at any price. But we have to keep a cool head, and preparations must be carried out with attention to every detail."

That first hint of encouragement from the Under Secretary, fragile as it was, supplied Moccagatta with all he needed to begin preliminary action. Within hours, he had ordered a group of E-boats dispatched to the big Sicilian naval base at Augusta. And before the week was out, he was leading a pair of scout boats on a night-approach to the coast of Malta, to check the sensitivity of the British defenses and the vulnerability of Grand Harbor's entrance. He made two such runs, and logged them in his diary:

"Augusta, 25 May — Put out to sea. After doubling Cape Passero, the weather became so bad that I had to reduce speed from 30 knots to 18.

"Consequently we arrived on station, four miles off Grand Harbor, nearly two hours late. A dark war-time night.

"I remained on the lookout for about two hours without sighting anything of interest. A few searchlights flashed and a British aircraft landed, but that was all. At 7:30 a.m. I was back in the harbor at Augusta."

"Augusta, 28 May — Tonight I went out with the two motorboats again, to the lookout station off Valletta. The night was dark and overcast, a long swell running.

"There was nothing to see — only three air raids between 3:30 and 4:30, the last of which gave a clear illumination of the entire area for several seconds.

"I have been informed by telephone that, in view of the few targets present at Malta, the Supreme Command does not consider it timely to take action. I shall return to Rome and renew my arguments for the operation."

Whatever arguments Moccagatta may have advanced for his project have not been recorded. But they must have been powerful and persuasive. The fact is that he left Rome and returned to Sicily on June 23 carrying executive orders from Supermarina authorizing the Malta attack. He was to have a free hand.

"This will be the great chance!" he announced to Giorgio Giobbe on his return to Augusta.

But Giobbe remained unconvinced, and didn't hesitate to make known his doubts and uneasiness about the whole plan of action. He spent the better part of two days trying to persuade Moccagatta to call the whole thing off.

"I have listened to him attentively," Moccagatta wrote in his diary. "Giobbe keeps telling me over and over again that he is extremely dubious about the success of the operation. He stubbornly refuses to see it any differently.

"But I have no doubts at all. So I tell him that his job right now is simply to hurry up and get the detailed orders ready."

On several more nights, then, Moccagatta carried out further reconnaissance missions off Valletta. Each time, he took with him several members of the assault teams, to familiarize them with conditions near the harbor area. On one such occasion, while at sea, he received a radio warning from Rome to be on the alert for a British convoy of one battleship, one aircraft carrier, 14 destroyers and 14 merchant ships, reportedly steaming toward Malta from the direction of Gibraltar.

"That would make an interesting night of it," he remarked to Giobbe.

Giobbe did not reply, and the convoy did not come into sight.

Finally, with preparations at maximum level, the attack was set for the night of July 25-26. According to the forecast, the weather would be calm and the new moon just right.

On the night of the 23rd, Moccagatta went out on his final reconnaissance mission. He returned with a heavy feeling of weariness, worn down by tensions and by the long days and nights of physical commitment. Also, for the first time, he was feeling vaguely troubled by a nagging sense of doubt that he could not quite explain. He blamed his feelings on extreme fatigue, and mentioned them just briefly in his diary:

"I got back this morning at 7:30. So far as the motorboats were concerned — that is, our two patrol boats — everything went off well, as I got to within 2000 meters of Malta and identified the buoys marking the entrance channels. As for the E-boats themselves, though, I came back feeling somewhat discouraged and concerned. The Malta coast is extremely difficult to reconnoiter in the dark. There is always a considerable current running east, and consequently the position of the boats for the start of the attack will be subject to miscalculation. This could cause great trouble.

"Moreover, the enemy must have heard me, for they switched on four powerful searchlights, scanning in my direction…"

He was wrong; the enemy had not heard him. They had been watching him, tracking his every move on a radar network that had just been installed at Valletta.

Chapter 13.
Two Minutes to Disaster

The sun was setting on the 25th of July as the assault group assembled at Augusta for its attack on Malta.

Conditions for the operation were excellent. The sea was calm, almost mirror-like. Not a trace of wind disturbed the warm, summery air. The coming night promised to be gentle and moonless. And air reconnaissance had reported a large convoy of merchant ships at anchor in Grand Harbor.

The destroyer *Diana* which had formerly been used by Mussolini as a private yacht, had arrived in port at Augusta five days earlier and was now the center of activity for departure preparations. Nine E-boats from River Serchio had been placed aboard her deck. These she would carry to a point off Malta, where she would launch them for attack.

In addition, she would tow a special MTL motorboat that would carry human-torpedoes. Accompanying her would be two more motorboats, the MAS-451 and MAS-452, carrying Moccagatta and the Tenth Flotilla's special doctor, Captain Bruno . Also in line would be an MTSM torpedo-motorboat with Giorgio Giobbe aboard, assigned to guide the E-boats to the entrance of Grand Harbor, send them on their way, and later pick up survivors. Since there would be no role in the operation for the submarine *Scire,* Prince Borghese had been ordered to remain behind at La Spezia.

Of the two human-torpedoes, one was under command of Teseo Tesei, with P.O. diver Alcide Pedretti assisting. Tesei's mission would be to blow apart a steel-net barrier that hung beneath St. Elmo Bridge, blasting open a path for the E-boats to rush into Grand Harbor and attack ships at anchor. The assignment for the second human-torpedo, carrying Lieutenant Franco Costa and diver Luigi Barla, would be to veer sharply to the right from Tesei's course and enter Marsa Muscetto Bay, just a few hundred yards west of Grand Harbor; and there to attack a nest of moored British submarines.

Meanwhile the timetable had been set with careful attention to synchronization. The Air Force had agreed to launch three diversionary raids. At 1:45 a.m. on the 26th, there would be an air attack against Valletta, designed not only to distract the British but also to prod the searchlights into action, thus helping the attackers at sea to home in on their target. At 2:30, a heavier air raid on Valletta would further disrupt the British defenses. At 4:30, Italian planes would hit Malta's inland airfield at Mikabba, diverting attention from Grand Harbor itself.

And also at 4:30 — exactly at zero hour — the explosion of Tesei's torpedo attacking the barrier at St. Elmo Bridge would signal the instant for unleashing the assault boats.

"It must come at precisely 4:30," Moccagatta had cautioned."Any earlier, it will be too dark for the boats to see where they're going. Any later, too light to escape detection. At exactly 4:30, the nets must be blown and the boats must rush in."

Tesei had listened calmly. "At 4:30 on the dot, I guarantee you'll hear it."

So now at Augusta, with daylight ending, the boats of the Flotilla settled into position, and each man stood ready at his post, poised for the start of the southward journey to Malta. The sun had dipped into the sea, its final glow flashing like a signal beam. Aboard the *Diana*, a flag hoist soared aloft to ripple from a yardarm. A rumble came from the destroyer's engine room, and the ship's deck began to quiver. Without further fuss, the Flotilla got under way.

Some hours later, at 10:30 that night, the "All Stop" signal rang down from the *Diana*'s bridge to the engine room, and the ship slowed to a halt. The crossing from Augusta had gone smoothly, without incident. The destroyer lay to, riding gently on the sea, just 20 miles from the darkened entrance to Grand Harbor.

One by one the *Diana* lowered the explosive E-boats overside and set them afloat to test engines. One of the nine refused to respond, and was immediately and quietly sunk. The others, led by Giobbe in his motor-torpedo boat, moved into line-ahead formation and set out at slow speed toward the island. They were escorted by the MS-451 and MS-452, and by the boat carrying the two human-torpedoes.

Giobbe glanced at his watch.

It was almost an hour to midnight. He nodded approvingly, estimating that their arrival at a point some 2000 yards off St. Elmo Bridge would take place right on schedule, at about 3 a.m. A glance astern showed him that the *Diana* had turned and already was fading into the shadows, heading back toward Augusta. He adjusted his boat's speed, to hold the Flotilla steady at a quiet 5 knots. Then he leaned back and relaxed; for the moment, at least, the operation was going well.

What neither Giobbe nor Moccagatta nor anybody else in the attack group knew, however, was that at that moment operations on Malta were also going well. At exactly 10:30 P.M., as the *Diana* had signaled "All Stop", the British radar plot at Valletta had revealed an unidentified surface force approaching the island. The radar operators had zeroed in on the telltale blips, following the whole procedure with alert care. They had seen a large craft halt for a time, then turn and move away in the direction of Sicily. They had seen the others slide into column formation and begin to move toward Valletta — eight of them — ten of them — eleven. The screen monitored their approach with perfect precision.

Quickly but quietly, the alarm was relayed to all defense units on the island. At the airfield, Swordfish aircraft were alerted and made ready for takeoff at dawn. All four main batteries guarding Grand Harbor and Marsa Muscetto Bay were manned and made ready for action. At Fort St. Elmo, at Ricasoli, at Punta Rocco and at Tigne, darkened searchlights and powerful guns alike were trained and adjusted for a crossfire concentration on the St. Elmo channel entrance.

Then the British sat back and waited, watching their radar track the steady approach of the oncoming surface force.

The Flotilla had reached a point within a mile of the harbor entrance when Giobbe signaled a halt. He waited there for several minutes, alert, scanning the coast through night-glasses and straining his ears for some sign of detection on the part of the enemy. He heard nothing, saw nothing. All was dark and still. Then, as planned for this stage, he ordered the E-boats and all other craft to hold back, while the MTL transport motorboat with the two human-torpedoes crept on ahead.

Aboard the MTL, Tesei ordered an approach to within 1000 yards of St. Elmo Bridge. There, he and Costa supervised the unloading of their torpedoes and climbed aboard with their divers to test engines. It was exactly 3 a.m. Tesei noted the time, remarking to himself that he had 90 minutes in which to make his approach and blow the St. Elmo barrier. A good, safe margin, he reflected. He wondered, idly, what had gone wrong with the plan for diversionary air raids. The initial raid on Valletta, scheduled for 1:45, had not taken place at all. The heavier raid, set for 2:30, had consisted only of a solitary plane making a single bombing run over the city at 2:45. He shrugged; obviously they'd be getting no help from that direction. He turned his attention to his torpedo engine and switched on the ignition. It exploded into life instantly. He throttled it down, satisfied.

Costa, though, was having trouble. His torpedo engine was skipping erratically, and his ballast pump had jammed. Unable to get moving, he appealed to Tesei for help, and together the two men worked frantically in the dark, trying to get the torpedo in trim and make it maneuverable. Meanwhile the minutes ticked on, with each instant cutting away the margin of time in which Tesei might reach the barrier, set his explosive fuse for 4:30, and get safely out of the blast area.

At 3:45, Tesei ran out of time. He grasped Costa's hand for a farewell shake. "I'll have to go," he said. "If I wait any longer, the boats will be trapped by the sunrise."

"Go ahead, take off," said Costa. "I'll do what I can with this cripple. At least we've got her moving now. With luck I might make it. But Teseo — don't do anything foolish. If it looks too dangerous at the net — if you don't have time to get away — turn back. We need you alive, not dead."

Tesei got astride his torpedo. "I've just got time to reach the net by 4:30, and that's about all. But at 4:30, that net will blow up. That's all that matters. Good-bye, Franco. Good luck."

With a wave of his hand, he eased open his throttle and disappeared in the darkness, angling his craft down out of sight beneath the surface. In his mind he knew he had no choice; if the net was to blow on time, he and Pedretti must blow up with it. There was no other way.

And as Tesei disappeared, Costa mounted his faulty vehicle and moved off slowly in the direction of Marsa Muscetto. He could not submerge. But at least, he reasoned, he might stay hidden by the shadows. The important thing was to try.

Meanwhile on the E-boats, the assault-men drew their craft close to Giobbe's motor-torpedoboat and followed him on a cautious approach that brought them ever closer to the bridge. It was 4 a.m., then 4:15. The harbor area was silent. The outlines of the bridge structure took shape dimly in the darkness ahead. Giobbe brought the boats to a halt and eased his craft down the line from one to the other, giving each man a handshake in passing. He spoke to them softly:. "Frassetto, Carabelli, Bosio, Zaniboni, Pedrini, Follieri, Marchisio, Capriotti. Only minutes to go, now. Frassetto, you take the lead. Then Carabelli. If the net is still in the way, blow it open. Then Bosio — you lead the others through. Remember your orders — that seven men must sacrifice themselves, if necessary, to clear the way for one. But clear it at all costs!"

He glanced at his watch. "It's coming up on 4:30. First light, in just a few moments. Stand by now. Wait for Tesei's signal."

At that instant, it came. The sea shuddered with the shock of a violent underwater explosion. Tesei had done his job.

"Go!" yelled Giobbe.

The boats took off in a burst of foam and a roar of engines. They raced across the sea at top speed. Out in front, Frassetto and Carabelli headed straight for the bridge. Eighty yards from the net, Frassetto locked his rudder and hurled himself overboard. Carabelli roared on, clinging to his boat, a suicidal projectile racing headlong for the main bridge abutment. He slammed into it with a thundering explosion that hurled metal and flesh high into the air.

But he had done too well. With a grinding screech, the whole span crashed into the sea, completely blocking the entrance.

Simultaneously, batteries of searchlights lit up the area like daylight and the harbor defense guns opened fire. The six onrushing E-boats, with Bosio in the lead, were caught in a blinding maze of light beams. Shells roared down upon them in a devastating crossfire. Machine guns, Bofors guns and 140-millimeter cannon poured a storm of destruction upon the trapped and blinded assault-men, pinning them in a helpless, swirling confusion of death, blood and wreckage.

It ended as quickly as it had begun. In two minutes, there was nothing left to shoot at. The guns went silent. The searchlights stared down on a scene where nothing moved.

From his position at sea, half hidden in the weak light of dawn, Giobbe had watched the swift holocaust from its start to its quick finish. It sickened him, left him sobbing and retching with his head hanging over the rail of his boat. Finally recovering, he sat still for several long minutes, waiting without hope for some sign of a returning survivor. But none appeared. Those who had not been killed outright would spend the rest of the war as prisoners.

At last, as the searchlights one by one went dark, Giobbe got his boat under way and turned back to follow the 451 and 452, which were already proceeding slowly away toward Sicily. He overtook them in less than half an hour, and went aboard the 452 to make his bitter report to Moccagatta. Prudently, Moccagatta took Giobbe's boat in tow and immediately ordered top speed for the long run home.

But top speed was not enough. One hour later, with daylight spreading brightly across the sea, the Swordfish and Hurricane planes from Malta came tearing after the boats like swarms of angry hornets, raking them again and again with machine gun fire. Quickly, Italian Macchi planes raced out from Sicily to battle the Hurricanes. But the British shot down three of them and drove off the others.

The first slashing air attack on the 452 killed Giobbe, Moccagatta, Falcomata and three of the crew. The second attack killed two more men and ripped open the boat's hull. Eleven survivors leaped across to Giobbe's craft, cut the towline and sped away in pursuit of the Diana which by now was nearing home.

Meanwhile aboard the 451, gunfire from the attacking planes hit the fuel tanks and set the boats ablaze. A burst of fire from the boat's machine gun brought down one British plane, but then the boat exploded with a violent roar, instantly killing four seamen.

Nine survivors, most of them wounded, were plucked from the sea some six hours later by a British patrol craft from Malta. On the return trip to Valletta, they passed the crippled 452, silent and lifeless with her cargo of dead men.

Of the attack force that had left Augusta, then, only broken remnants remained. The only survivors who escaped were the 11 men from the 452, who had used Giobbe's swift boat to overtake the *Diana*. The total losses for the Italians consisted of 15 men killed, 18 taken prisoner, one motorboat sunk, one motorboat captured, nine E-boats sunk, two human-torpedoes lost, along with their transport boat, and three Macchi fighter planes shot down. The British, meanwhile, had lost one aircraft. In all, it was the bloodiest and costliest attack ever to be undertaken by the men from River Serchio.

Back in Rome, on the day following the debacle, a friend of Teseo Tesei received a letter dated July 17. Tesei had signed it and posted it just before embarking for Malta. It said:

"By the time you receive this letter, I shall have attained the highest of all honors — that of giving my life for my King and my Flag. This is the supreme desire of a soldier, the most sublime joy he can experience..."

He had known his role from the beginning.

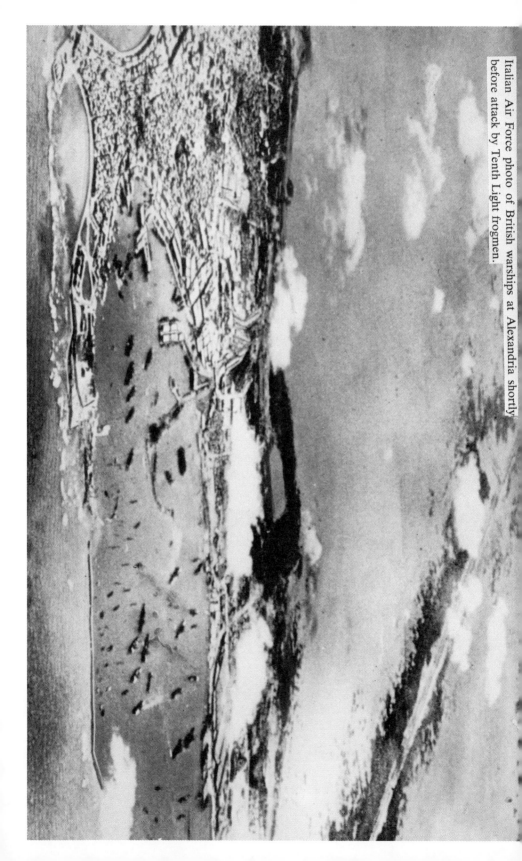

Italian Air Force photo of British warships at Alexandria shortly before attack by Tenth Light frogmen.

Chapter 14.
Pause For Recovery

In terms of both men and equipment, the springtime victory at Suda Bay had been costly, the summertime defeat at Malta disastrous. For the moment, then, no further operations could be initiated from River Serchio until the Tenth Light had been restored to good health and put back in fighting trim. There were jagged holes to be plugged, men to be replaced, spirits to be renewed.

Supermarina moved quickly to accomplish all this by naming Borghese to be temporary Commanding Officer of the Flotilla, succeeding the dead Moccagatta.

"A great honor," Borghese wrote in his journal, "especially in view of my rank (Lieutenant Commander).

"To replace the gallant Giobbe, I have given the command of the Surface Division to an officer of the highest personal and professional qualifications, a friend whose career has run parallel to my own. He is Lieutenant Commander Salvatore Todaro, the hero of epic gun fights in the Atlantic, where he was in command of the submarine *Cappellini*.

"I am devoting myself almost entirely to the Underwater Division, which I keep in my own hands. I intend to take advantage of the summer season while it lasts. It is unsuitable for human-torpedo operations, owing to the shortness of the nights and the length of the hours of daylight; but it is favorable (because of sea temperatures) for intensive and prolonged training. Therefore the veteran pilots of Serchio and the recruits who are now coming in, full of the enthusiasm of neophytes, are being put through the most concentrated and rigorous training exercises. They are responding very well.

"At the same time, I have availed myself of the quiet, steady and effective work of a gifted talented officer, Naval Engineer Major Mario Masciulli, from the secret torpedo works placed at our disposal by the Underwater Weapons Board at La Spezia."

It turned out to be a winning combination.

Borghese, pulling all strings available, quickly convinced the Naval Ministry at Rome that the Tenth should have its own fleet of transportation ships, ready on an instant's notice to carry assault-teams from La Spezia to designated target areas. Rome agreed, and assigned him the armed trawlers *Cefalo*, *Sogliola*, and *Costanza* ,plus a new submarine, the *Ambra*. These, added to his submarine *Scire*, gave the Tenth a built-in fleet readiness to move its weapons at will to any action area in the Mediterranean.

Todaro, displaying remarkable talents of leadership psychology, soon had his surface teams well tuned and impatient for a chance to get into combat. He followed this up by making personal visits to the factory owners who were turning out material for the Tenth, and persuading them to speed up production. They complied, and the new weapons began to flow.

Masciulli meanwhile familiarized himself with the weakness of the Toschi-Tesei type of human torpedo and set out to design an improved model. He struck almost instant success, thereby giving the Tenth the most deadly arsenal it had ever possessed.

Then in early August, fresh instructions from Supermarina arrived on Borghese's desk at River Serchio:

"Step up preparations to destroy enemy ships in harbor and to interdict enemy supply lines. To that end, expand recruitment and accelerate training soonest possible."

In the Underwater Division, Borghese reacted by establishing a new branch of assault swimmers known as the "Gamma Group." These frogmen, aided by rubber fins and breathing masks, were trained to make individual sorties against moored merchant ships, and to attach special explosive devices and time-fuse detonators to the ship's hull. Each man was trained to work alone at night, camouflaged by blackened face, and to reach his target by swimming underwater with just his eyes above the surface. He would approach the selected ship bow-on, drifting slowly with the current or with whatever surface-flow held the ship in position. He would attach his device near the vessel's propeller shaft. He would then ease off and let the current carry him out of sight in the darkness astern. A special training school for this underwater group was established at the Naval Academy at Leghorn, with a friend of Borghese's, Lieutenant Eugenio Wolk in command.

Inevitably the new expanded programs called for more and more recruits. But the Tenth Light still had to be highly selective in its choice of men; it needed volunteers of spirit, nerve, reliability and courage, but also it needed men of top skill as swimmers. And to locate such candidates as quickly as possible, Borghese called upon the prestigious Italian Swimmers League to help out by supplying him with the names on its membership list.

To his astonishment, he discovered that most of the best swimmers in Italy had already been tabbed by the government for duty in the Army, not in the Navy where they belonged. They were both willing and eager to join the "Gamma Group" and to fight the war at sea. But as it turned out, some of them were slogging through mud as infantrymen on the Russian Front, some were riding tanks in the heat and dust of North Africa, and some were even perched on craggy mountains, fighting in the ranks of the Alpine Troops.

The problem of straightening out this bureaucratic tangle, and getting the best swimmers into the water, landed in the lap of Supermarina. Emergency calls went out immediately to the Ministry of War. And for once, the traditional rivalries between Army and Navy were swept aside with good grace; within a few brief days, Italy's finest young swimmers began arriving at River Serchio to be processed for duty with the Tenth Light. They were delighted with their change of orders.

Finally, by the first week in September, all programs under Borghese's command were filled to quota and running smoothly. His paperwork and groundwork at last lay behind him; now there was a war to be fought at sea.

In this mood, one late-summer evening, he went out to stroll by himself along the quiet Serchio riverbank and to evaluate his position. It was a time for review and assessment, for taking a long look at what the Tenth had been through in the past twelve months and at the demands that might arise in the months ahead.

He walked slowly, pausing for lengthy intervals to stare reflectively at the Serchio pools, pondering the past and the future alike while listening to the sounds of night creatures in the woods around him. He sensed that the Tenth had reached a critical turning point. The year just past had been bloody and harsh. Good men had been lost, and good ships also. The *Iride* and the *Gondar*, gone in tragic sinkings. Many brave men like Toschi, Giorgini, Faggioni, Cabrini and their shipmates were now in the prison camps of the enemy. Gallant men like Tesei, Pedretti, Moccagatta, Carabelli — all dead.

There had been terrible defeats and disappointments, with only the victory at Suda Bay to credit the record. And yet, he reflected, there was far more to the story than just the Suda triumph. The men of the Tenth had won in important other respects as well. For now, after a year of trial and bitter loss, of mistakes and correction, they had emerged with hard-won experience and self-confidence. Surely that was the biggest victory of all. The Tenth, he told himself, was now a strong fighting unit, skilled at its job, armed with reliable weapons and the ability to use them, and armed also with an enthusiastic determination to sink enemy shipping wherever it might be attacked. The Flotilla had been at war for over a year, but most of its fighting had been against its own handicaps. Now, that was all over. Now at last, he felt, the assault-teams were ready to unleash crippling blows against the enemy. Yes, he was sure of it. And the more he sat thinking about it, watching the flow of the Serchio, the more confident he became.

Later that evening, back in his quarters, Borghese sat alone at his desk to bring his journal up to date.

"The nights are growing long now," he wrote. "It is time to take the Scire back to Gibraltar."

Chapter 15.
To Cadiz for Briefing

In September of 1941, the Italian tanker *Fulgor* lay at anchor in the harbor of Cadiz, close to where the River Guadalete flowed down from the Spanish hills to meet the sea. She had been interned there for fifteen months, ever since the hour of Italy's entry into the war.

Ordinarily, life aboard the *Fulgor* was dull and wearisome. As the months had gone by, Spanish authorities and British espionage agents alike had casually lost interest in her. They were content with the fact that the Italian officers and crewmen aboard went quietly about their necessary care-taking duties and made no attempt to put to sea. The *Fulgor*, in fact, had become a familiar part of their normal harbor scenery, and as such had blended into her surroundings so effectively as to be almost totally ignored by routine patrols and waterfront observers.

But now the *Fulgor* was to take on a new mission in life, albeit in such a quiet and unobtrusive way as to arouse no curiosity on the part of enemy agents, either afloat or ashore. She was to become a clandestine rendezvous point and briefing station for River Serchio assault-teams intent on attacking Gibraltar.

The plan, conceived by Borghese, was a simple one. The assault-teams, in disguise, would be flown from Italy to Cadiz and transported to the *Fulgor* posing as replacement deckhands or repair crews, or on some equally plausible pretext. Meanwhile the submarine *Scire*, carrying weapons and attack gear, would make the trip from La Spezia to the Straits of Gibraltar, travel submerged into the Atlantic, surface near Cape Tarifa and proceed north to Cadiz, entering the harbor under cover of darkness. Once inside the harbor, she would go alongside the *Fulgor* and moor there semi-submerged, virtually camouflaged from the casual eye. The *Fulgor* then would become the departure point for operations against ships at Gibraltar.

The plan went into action. On the evening of September 10, Borghese stood bare-headed in the breeze on the *Scire*'s conning tower bridge and watched the dim shoreline of La Spezia blend into the shadows falling away astern. He felt relieved to be back at sea again, glad of the prospect of returning to action. He gave his orders quietly before going below to check his charts: "All ahead full...Run surfaced for five minutes. Then take her down to 100 feet and level off for tests. Then bring her up for surface running."

The tests were carried out efficiently and without a hitch. For the rest of the night, then, the *Scire* ran southwestward down the Ligurian Sea, a slender shadow moving under the starlight.

Six nights later, Borghese took the *Scire* through the Straits of Gibraltar at a running depth of 200 feet and passed safely from the Mediterranean into the Atlantic. At dawn on the 17th, off the mouth of Cadiz Harbor, he put his ship gently on the bottom in 130 feet of water, to wait out the hours of daylight.

It was a long, relaxing day, spent at rest in the peaceful darkness of the deep. It gave Borghese a chance to catch up on his private journal:

"There is nothing more relaxing than to be in a submarine at rest on the bottom of the sea," he wrote. "The hushed silence that comes with being submerged is intensified by the total absence of any mechanical sound aboard. A man feels safe from all interruption, well sheltered by the water above and all around. There is a sense of being at home in a protective world which nobody can find, much less penetrate.

"Today I am remembering another time when hours were spent like this. It was Christmas Eve in 1937, and we were on patrol in the

Spanish War. My submarine then was the *Iride*, and we were off the harbor of Tarragona somewhat south of Barcelona. We were planning a midnight celebration of the holy day, and the crew had made the ship ready for the occasion by constructing a special Christmas Tree. Its trunk was a broomstick, its pine needles were green-painted straw, and its illumination came from colored light bulbs. They had also put together a traditional crib, with Nativity figures cut from the tops of empty tin cans — and a figure of the Christ Child baked in dough.

"On Christmas Day, I brought the *Iride* close to the harbor entrance and took her up to periscope depth, training our glass on the decorated shore-line and the beautiful Tarragona Cathedral. Then I had everyone aboard take turns looking through the periscope, for if we could not visit a church on this day at least we could look at one. We talked for a while of other Christmas celebrations, and of our friends and families, and then we brought the periscope down and submerged to the bottom again. That night the crew surprised me by serving up a splendid Christmas feast, complete with songs and wine and a holiday cake."

Finished with his reminiscing, he then wrote a brief entry for the official log:

"17 September, 0600. Submerged 8 miles, 90 degrees bearing, from Cadiz Lighthouse. Remained on bottom, depth 40 meters, until nightfall.

"Assembled crew.Informed them first phase of operation (voyage) now over, and briefed them on second phase (attack on Gibraltar). After this, all hands rested."

As the night came down, cloaking Cadiz in shadows, the *Scire* surfaced and glided quietly into the harbor. She crossed the open water undetected and moored alongside the *Fulgor*, well hidden in the darkness cast upon the tide by the tanker's hull. Borghese went aboard immediately, to be given a warm greeting by the ship's officers and escorted to the wardroom.

It was a welcome break from routine. To men accustomed to the cramped quarters of a submarine, the *Fulgor* seemed almost like a floating hotel. It was spacious, comfortable and well ventilated. It offered a chance to get a hot shower and a shave without knocking elbows and knuckles against the plumbing. It had deep armchairs, where a man could sit and sprawl his feet without tripping up a shipmate. Instead of canned, dried rations on a shelf, there were bowls of fresh fruit on the wardroom tables. White-jacketed stewards moved about, serving wine from Jerez and cigars from Havana. Borghese promptly sent back word to the *Scire* to have his men come aboard in groups of four, to enjoy a taste of the good life while they had the chance. Then he turned to the business at hand, to the pre-attack conference on Gibraltar.

Awaiting his words, and enjoying all the comforts of the wardroom, were the members of the assault-teams, flown in from River Serchio. One by one they shook his hand and drew their chairs around him, bringing their wine and cigars to the table. He checked their names against his clipboard roster, and proceeded at once with the briefing.

"This is it," he said crisply. "Here's the lineup. The three teams for direct attack will be Lieutenant Decio Catalano and diver Giuseppe Giannoni — Lieutenant Amedeo Vesco and diver Antonio Zozzoli — Lieutenant Licio Visintini and diver Giovanni Magro. For the reserve team, Engineer Antonio Marceglia and diver Spartaco Schergat. The surgeon-physician for the operation, you all know Lieutenant Giorgio Spaccarelli. And I hope you find nothing to do but read books, Giorgio."

"Good thinking," said the doctor. "I brought some along."

"Most of you have been on these missions before," Borghese went on, "and each of you asked for the chance to be on this one. When I approved your requests, I added the comment that I'm confident you'll succeed — that you're the best in the business. Please don't let me down."

The men murmured self-consciously, leaning forward to listen.

"Now, for the timetable." Borghese paused to straighten his papers. "We will go aboard the Scire at midnight and leave the harbor shortly before dawn. I plan to enter Algeciras Bay at nightfall on the 19th — forty-eight hours from now — and proceed to our selected station off the River Guadarranque. The attack-teams will depart from the submarine at 0100 on the 20th — and the Scire will head back for La Spezia. After completing your mission and making your way to the shore, you will be met near La Linea by agent 'P' who will arrange for your flight back to Italy. Any questions so far?"

"I have a question," said Visintini. "Have the British come up with any new defensive tactics we should know about?"

"Only that they seem to be getting more wary," Borghese replied. "By now they have a pretty good idea of what to watch out for. They know we have E-boats, they know about the human-torpedoes. So, they have brought in new motorboats for patrol duties, and apparently these boats are powered by electric motors that run almost silently. They cruise around the harbor all night and drop depth charges every half-hour or so. They're difficult to detect. They move like shadows. Keep a sharp lookout for them. Anything more?"

"When do we get our target information?" Vesco asked.

"Don't be impatient," said Borghese. "You'll get it right now. And take my word, there's plenty to pick from.

"According to the latest radio from Rome tonight, Gibraltar is getting crowded. On hand, there's a battleship of the Nelson class, an aircraft carrier, two cruisers, seven naval tankers and three destroyers, all in the inner harbor. Meanwhile, seventeen merchant ships are anchored in the roadstead."

Visintini gave a soft whistle. "How can we miss?"

"You shouldn't," said Borghese. "It's a setup. Now then, Rome will contact the Scire again on the night of the 19th, after we arrive on station. At that time we'll be advised of the exact anchorage positions of the big ships, and you'll be given your final target assignments. Tentatively, I'd say that the Vesco and Catalano teams will attack the battleship, and Visintini will go in after the aircraft carrier."

The men sipped their wine and nodded silent approval.

"But — and this is very important," Borghese went on. "If you find you can't hit the warships, don't waste the whole night on them. Select another target and attack, before it's too late.

"And always remember," he continued, "warships may be important, but the fact remains that the enemy cannot fight an action without the necessary supplies from its tankers and cargo ships. They are vitally important. Take them away and the enemy is paralyzed. So, if the fighting ships are out of your reach — if there's no way of attacking them — sink the biggest targets you can find, no matter what. Do that, and you'll go home a winner.

"That's all I have to say," he concluded. "Now let's relax with our drinks and swap lies like good Navymen until it's time to go aboard the Scire."

Chapter 16.
Victory at Gibraltar

The slow sad tones of a distant church bell striking midnight echoed across Algeciras Bay as the *Scire* rose to the surface, exactly on schedule. Borghese went up the ladder and through the hatch to the bridge. Quickly he adjusted his night-binoculars and leaned against the rail, taking a full-circle view of the surrounding water. Satisfied, he stepped back to the hatch and softly called below.

"All clear. Come on up."

One by one, Vesco, Visintini and Catalano emerged from below and joined him, all wearing their underwater gear. They stared around them in the darkness, noting the position of the flickering lights of La Linea to the east, Algeciras to the southwest, and Gibraltar's Grand Harbor anchorage to the southeast..

"It's black," said Vesco. "The nights get blacker all the time. Perhaps I imagine it."

"And rough," said Visintini. "We've got a strong easterly breeze and a choppy sea. That means lots of waves in our faces."

"Look at it this way — it's even blacker down below," said Borghese. "But no waves down there anyhow. So, has everybody got his bearings?"

Catalano nodded. "All set, skipper."

"You've got your anchorage positions from Rome Radio," said Borghese. "You've got your target assignments. Vesco and Catalano — you leave in fifteen minutes, at 12:30. Visintini, you go right after that. The agent 'P' will be waiting for you on the La Linea shore road at 6 a.m. And by last count, you've got 31 ships to choose from. Let's make it a big night. Ready to go?"

"Just give us our farewell kick," said Vesco. "Can't leave without that."

Solemnly, one by one, they bent forward in the darkness. And just as solemnly, Borghese booted each man in turn.

"My pleasure," he said. "Also, my privilege. Good luck, now. And God bless you."

"And good luck to you," they replied. "Safe voyage home."

Ten minutes later, Vesco and Zozzoli slipped away from the hull of the submarine, riding astride their torpedo, heading for the distant lights of the Gibraltar anchorage and keeping their senses alert for any sign of cruising patrol boats. Catalano and Giannoni followed within moments. Visintini and Magro then glided away, leaving the *Scire* alone in the darkness of the bay.

Borghese made a final sweep with his night-glasses, and took a bearing on the lights of Gibraltar. Then he went below, sealing the watertight hatch behind him. He took the *Scire* down to a depth of 80 feet and leveled off.

"Both engines slow ahead," he ordered. "Course two-oh-five."

"...Steady on two-oh-five, sir."

He relaxed against the chart table and took a slow drink of coffee. His part of the operation was over. Now for the long journey home to La Spezia.

As the submarine moved down toward the Straits, the two-man attack teams on the surface were coping doggedly with individual problems that threatened for a time to disrupt the whole mission. They had scarcely left the *Scire* before they lost contact with each other in the darkness. Rough seas and a brisk wind kept slapping the waves against their face masks, salting their eyes and blurring their vision. Now and then they choked on sea water. Their torpedoes bucked and rolled.

After a two-hour struggle, Vesco and Zozzoli arrived in calmer waters at a point less than 150 yards from the Grand Harbor defenses. There Vesco cut his engines and hove to on the surface, sizing up his surroundings. Shore lights glistened in the near background, bringing into relief the outlines of ships and breakwaters. A patrol boat, cruising back and forth at the harbor entrance, curved toward him in a wide, sweeping arc. He submerged silently, holding at 85 feet down until the boat had passed overhead. Then he moved forward at low speed, his torpedo occasionally scraping the hard, smooth surface of the channel bed.

.Minutes later he felt the heavy jar of three underwater explosions, followed closely by two more. These would be random depth charges, he told himself; probably from the patrol boat guarding the entrance. He checked his watch and his instruments; the time was 3:40, and he was suspended at a depth of 45 feet. He surfaced cautiously, to find that he was now little more than 50 yards from the harbor entrance. He could see clearly the looming silhouette of a battleship, moored behind the protective bulk of the south breakwater. But he could also see the lights of a British patrol craft that had taken station directly in his path, making it impossible to penetrate the anchorage without being discovered. Regretfully he turned away, setting out to find a new target among the ships anchored in the roadstead.

It was close to 5 a.m. by the time he and Zozzoli had completed their work. They had chosen for destruction the *Fiona Shell,* a tanker of about 4,000 tons, riding low and obviously fully laden. They had attached their 500-pound explosive charge to the ship's hull, directly in line with the stack and the aft superstructure.

Vesco set the time fuse for a four-hour delay. He and Zozzoli then made their getaway, piloting their lightened torpedo-craft to a point just off La Linea, where they sank their vehicle and struck out for shore.

It was 7 a.m. when they finally crawled from the water and sprawled exhausted on the beach. Their sense of direction had been near-perfect, for they had arrived within 100 yards of their prearranged landing point. Their timing, though, was unfortunate, for they were spotted almost instantly from a distance by two Spanish border sentries, who greeted them by firing rifle shots into the air.

Hastily, they buried their diving suits and breathing gear in the sand, finishing the job just as the two sentries arrived on the spot.

The Spaniards held their rifles ready. "Identify yourselves!" they demanded.

Vesco shrugged. "We're Italian seamen," he explained. "We were shipwrecked last night. See — we have our papers." He reached for his waterproof folder.

The Spaniards waved it aside. "You are prisoners. You must come with us."

"Where? We have done nothing."

"Come with us, to the Coast Guard Station."

The station was only a short walk down the beach. Arriving there, Vesco was pleased to notice that it commanded a clear view of the *Fiona Shell*, riding at anchor in the distant roadstead, gleaming in the early morning sunlight. He was also pleased to notice that a smiling Italian civilian was waiting to greet them, the agent 'P' who had witnessed the entire capture scene from the beach road and had gone on ahead to the station to meet them with a pot of coffee.

'P' reached out with a handshake. "Your captors will be taken care of," he said. "We'll have you on a plane for Italy by noontime. How did it go?"

Vesco glanced at his wrist watch, then nodded toward the ships in the roadstead. "It looks peaceful out there, doesn't it? Watch what happens around 9 o'clock."

Meanwhile, Catalano and Giannoni also had been struggling through a night of trial and tension. They were scarcely two hours away from the *Scire*, laboring slowly toward the lights of Gibraltar, when Catalano sighted a British patrol boat some 75 yards to starboard, approaching quietly through the darkness. He stopped, then turned away on a widening course. The patrol boat followed, apparently tracking him by hydrophones. Again he turned, this time taking a course between two anchored merchant ships; and again the patrol boat followed, steadily closing the gap between them. Finally he submerged for a long wait under water.

It was 3:30 a.m. when he again broached the surface and took a careful look around. He sighed with relief; the patrol boat was gone. But with relief came also frustration, for the slow maneuvering and the long submersion had used up his margin of operating time. It would be useless now to try to reach the inner harbor and seek out a warship. There would be time now only to choose a target from among the vessels in the roadstead.

Moving from ship to ship in the darkness, then, Catalano first picked out a huge, empty tanker and signalled Giannoni to get to work. Giannoni had just finished attaching his explosive charge to the ship's propellers when Catalano noticed the name on the tanker's transom; she was the *Pollenzo*, out of Genoa, a captured ship in the service of the enemy.

He moved swiftly to Giannoni's side.

"Remove the charge, Giuseppe," he said. "We can't blow up Italian property. We'll have to look elsewhere."

Their second choice turned out to be a prize. She was the British motorship *Durham*, an armed vessel of 11,000 tons. She had just arrived in convoy, loaded to capacity with a cargo of high-explosive munitions. She rode low in the water, awaiting disposition of her bombs and shells and TNT.

Working smoothly and quickly, they fastened their heavy warhead to the *Durham*'s hull. With that done, Catalano set the four-hour time fuse and glanced at his watch; it was 5:16 as they pushed off for their underwater getaway. They made their withdrawal without incident, abandoning their vehicle 40 minutes later off the shore of La Linea and arriving on the beach at 7:15. Then they began trudging along the road in search of 'P'.

Similarly, Visintini and Magro had been fighting waves and eluding patrols ever since leaving the *Scire*. At 2:30 a.m., a darkened British patrol boat had passed within 300 feet of their craft. A half-hour later Visintini sighted the entrance to the anchorage and halted his approach to plan his next move. Twice he felt the jarring impact of depth charges, possibly from a dimly lit patrol boat that was moving nearby at two knots and turning slowly in his direction. He submerged, and waited for the boat to pass overhead. Then he surfaced once more and moved to a position directly in front of the harbor entrance. He glanced at his watch; it was 3:45.

The patrol boat that had been dogging him angled away gradually toward the south breakwater. Visintini watched it fade into the darkness, and then submerged to 35 feet to enter the anchorage at low speed. A defensive rigging of steel cables grazed his shoulders as he passed through the opening.

Inside, he surfaced again cautiously and removed his face mask for a better view of his surroundings. Almost immediately, he identified a Royal Navy cruiser at anchor some distance ahead of him and near the south end of the harbor. It would make a prime target, he knew; but the hour was now past 4 a.m., and he realized he would not have time to make his approach and attack the big ship. Also, he noted, she was ringed by cruising patrol boats that would make a successful attack almost impossible.

On the other hand, four big Royal Navy tankers were moored close by, tied up alongside the breakwater. They were riding low, carrying heavy cargoes of petrol. If he could blow up one of these, he reasoned, he might be able to set the whole harbor on fire. In fact, it might even cause more damage than blowing up the cruiser.

Satisfied, he chose what looked to be the biggest and heaviest ship of the lot. She was the *Denby Dale*, a 16,000-ton giant. Quietly he submerged to 30 feet and nudged his torpedo toward the tanker's hull. Occasionally he felt the shock of a distant depth charge, but these he ignored.

It was just 4:40 a.m. when he activated the time fuse on his warhead and pushed away to withdraw from the tanker's keel. For better or worse, the job was done. Two hours later, he and Magro rose from the sea off La Linea beach and walked ashore in the morning sunlight to look for 'P'.

At exactly 8:43, the *Denby Dale* blew up with a booming roar that rocked the harbor. Flames shot into the air, chunks of debris rained down, black smoke billowed aloft.

Gibraltar's anti-aircraft defense banged into action, firing blindly into the sky. Sirens screamed. Rescue craft rushed to the scene at top speed.

Seventeen minutes later, at the height of the confusion, the *Fiona Shell* exploded in the roadstead. She split in two in a shocking burst of flame. Her bow leaped out of the water, and she sank within minutes.

And at 9:16, with the harbor and the bay in blazing turmoil, the *Durham* erupted in the most terrible explosion of them all. A column of water shot 100 feet into the air. Sheets of flame shot up even higher. The thundering impact of thousands of tons of exploding munitions shattered window panes and shook buildings on shore for miles around.

The men from River Serchio, looking out from the Spanish Coast Guard Station, watched the fiery chaos with a pleased satisfaction. At long last, their training and their patience had paid off. And this, they knew, would be only the beginning. For this meant more than an isolated victory; it meant, in fact, that they had finally brought all their problems under control, and that from here on they would be a winning team.

In silent excitement, they stood staring out at the scene of destruction, until finally the agent 'P' broke their mood. "Come along, gentlemen," he urged them. "It's time to get to the air field."

Back in Rome, word of the Gibraltar victory arrived quickly at Supermarina and at the desk of Benito Mussolini. The news was promptly relayed to King Victor Emmanuel, who reacted by summoning Borghese to a royal audience at Quirinale Palace.

The King was in high spirits, and greeted Borghese warmly. "I understand you have been promoted to Commander," he said. "It's because of Gibraltar. I have a copy of your citation," He waved a rolled certificate.

"Yes, Your Majesty. I'm honored."

"It says here that you made the Gibraltar victory possible by your great ability and assiduous attention to detail — and it commends you for getting back safely to La Spezia, as it notes, 'despite difficulties due to determined pursuit by the enemy and to navigating under water, and driven to the limit of human endurance, thus providing a splendid example of organizing capacity and leadership.' Those are very brave words, and it's all here in this document. I congratulate you, Prince Borghese."

"Your Majesty is very kind."

"I have been hearing a great deal about the Tenth Flotilla," the King went on.

Borghese nodded. "We would hope so, Your Majesty. You know, our motto is 'Per il Re e la Bandiera'."

"For the King and Flag." The King smiled. "I am grateful. Tell me, what bothers you the most when you're down there in the Straits?"

"The currents," said Borghese. "The Gibraltar currents give me a lot more trouble than the Royal Navy."

Victor Emmanuel shook his head sympathetically. "How well I know! I took my wife fishing off Gibraltar once, and the currents were so terrible we never even caught a minnow."

"The Tenth Flotilla is luckier," Borghese replied. "We caught three big fish with no trouble at all."

The King laughed heartily. "I must learn to know more about the Tenth, for I think it will do great deeds. Tell me, Valerio — where do your men train for their wild kind of warfare?"

Borghese looked surprised. "I thought Your Majesty knew about that," he said. "We train at River Serchio, right at the edge of Your Majesty's San Rossore estate — on the estate of the Dukes of Salviati."

"That's astonishing news," said the King. "My own land, and I knew nothing about it. You keep your secrets in a most remarkable manner." He hesitated, and leaned forward. "Could I perhaps join you there next week, Valerio? I should like to meet your men and congratulate them personally. I'll pay my way by bringing a wild boar, and we'll celebrate with a barbecue. Would that be permitted?"

"Done, Your Majesty!" Borghese laughed. "We'd enjoy that!"

"Very well, then," said the King. "I'll be there four days from now. And now, one last thing, Valerio — if you can tell me. Where will the Tenth Flotilla strike the enemy next? Am I permitted to know?"

Borghese leaned toward him. "All I can say is this, Your Majesty," he replied. "After our victory at Gibraltar, we are inclined to believe that the English will very shortly remove their battleships to Alexandria. That should provide a most interesting development."

The King nodded, smiling. "Thank you, Valerio. And good luck with your fishing. We'll meet again at Serchio."

"Until then, Your Majesty. And good fishing for all of us."

Liberty ship from U.S., a frogman target at Gibraltar.

Chapter 17.
Focus Alexandria

Commander Ernesto Forza was a man who enjoyed the reputation of being one of the most popular and highly respected officers in the Italian Navy. He had built a brilliant record, studded with decorations for bravery in action. He was a skilled administrator with a special talent for outmaneuvering the guardians of bureaucracy. He had a sharp sense of humor.

He also, on this November day of 1941, had the grace and sensitivity to be feeling somewhat embarrassed. His problem was that he had been ordered from the Naval Base at Augusta to the base at La Spezia to relieve his good friend Borghese as Commanding Officer of the Tenth Light Flotilla. Upon his arrival, they discussed the change-of-command over wine and cigars in the Officers Club.

"What can I say about it?" Forza asked helplessly. "I was totally surprised. Your work has been brilliant. You're the talk of the Navy. Why should I be here?"

Borghese gave a friendly nod of reassurance. "You should be. And stop worrying. I made it clear to Supermarina that I'd welcome the change. My appointment to overall command was only temporary, to fill the gap left by the death of Moccagatta. Now with you here to run the show, I'm free to do what I really like best — to concentrate entirely on the underwater program, the human-torpedoes."

"Then you don't feel slighted?"

"On the contrary, I honestly feel pleased about it. But thanks for your concern."

Forza gestured with relief. "As usual then, you and I will get along in harmony."

"For King and Flag. Right?"

"And confusion to the English," said Forza. He sipped his wine. "Very well then, let's exchange ideas about what to do next. In view of the latest British casualties, I imagine that we're both contemplating the same target."

"I'm sure of it," Borghese agreed. "It has to be Alexandria. That's where we'll find the action."

"Correct. Then you know all about the British battleships and the sinking of the Barham?"

"In general but not in detail," said Borghese. "I just heard about it last night. Suppose you tell me exactly what happened."

Forza refilled his wine glass and leaned across the table. "It happened on the 25th, only two days ago. Just off the African coast, near Tobruk. It was just after 4 o'clock in the afternoon when a young German submarine skipper named Von Tiesenhausen brought his U-boat up to periscope depth for a look around and found himself staring at the kind of sight a submarine commander dreams about. Right out in front of him in broad daylight were all three battleships of the British Mediterranean Fleet, foaming along in line ahead, about 500 yards apart. God, what a picture that must have been!

"Leading the formation was Admiral Cunningham's flagship the Queen Elizabeth, then came the big Barham, then the Valiant. They were sweeping west with an escort of destroyers, probably hunting for one of our convoys.

"Anyhow, young Tiesenhausen promptly submerged and drove in at full speed, taking his U-boat right under the destroyer screen. A few minutes later he flipped up his periscope again, and there was the mighty Barham less than 500 yards away. *Down periscope!...Fire one!...Fire two!...*He cut loose with a full salvo of four torpedoes, and every damned one of them hit the mark. Two of them slammed right into her portside magazines!

"Well, the Barham went up like one huge bomb — one massive burst of smoke and flame, then whole sheets of armor plate raining down from the sky. It must have been like a scene out of Hades. They say the whole thing took only five minutes. The torpedoes struck home at 4:25. At 4:30 she had vanished from sight, and 900 seamen with her. The other ships managed to pick up about 500 survivors, which I'd say is a miracle in itself."

Borghese listened, taut with attention. "And Von Tiesenhausen? He got away?"

"He did," Forza replied. "He made his report to Doenitz yesterday morning. That's how we got our information."

"I see." Borghese thought for a bit. "Of course, the English won't acknowledge this for at least another month."

"Certainly not."

"But they'll be moving already to protect the ships that are left."

"Naturally," said Forza.

"So," said Borghese, "that plays to our advantage. The English realize that Gibraltar is not a safe place for the Royal Navy these days. My men sank three ships there just two months ago. And a U-boat sank the carrier Ark Royal there two weeks ago."

"Right."

"So as of this moment, Britain has only two battleships in the whole Mediterranean. And we have five. She'll guard her remaining two like an eagle guarding its eggs. But since she can't protect them at Gibraltar — ?"

"They'll be kept behind nets at Alexandria," Forza finished. "My thoughts exactly. When can you pay them a visit?"

Borghese took a slow drink of wine. "I've got it all planned out," he said. "Give us three weeks. Then we'll have some excitement."

Intensive preparation for the attack on Alexandria began at sunrise the next day. The crews that were chosen were veteran teams who had trained together for many months and had been together on previous missions — de la Penne with diver Bianchi, Marceglia with diver Schergat, and Martellotta with diver Marino, plus Spaccarelli and Feltrinelli in reserve.

Borghese assembled them later in the week for a briefing at River Serchio.

"Put all your affairs in order," he told them. "You may never return from this mission. If you survive, you'll probably be captured and spend a long term in the enemy's prison camps. Any comments on that?"

"Just send us a cake now and then," said de la Penne.

"Peace and good will," said Martellotta.

"We'll be working with the latest photos from air reconnaissance," Borghese went on. "We'll have complete information on hydrographic and weather conditions. The Scire has been given new radio channels for special security. New torpedoes are on their way from the works at San Bartolomeo. You'll be issued new swim-suits and breathing-gear. As usual, you won't be told where you're going until departure time."

The team captains nodded gravely. "Is it permitted to guess?" said Marceglia.

Borghese shook his head in mock reproof. "If you have to guess, you're in the wrong business. But it's too late to back out now.

"In any event, tomorrow is the third of December. Report aboard the Scire at 1400 hours. From then on, you'll be very busy men."

Twilight came early that next day, cloaking the harbor of La Spezia in a shroud of dusk. And as the shadows darkened the water, the *Scire* dropped her mooring lines and swung out toward the seaward channel, moving quietly and without flurry, as though departing on a normal patrol assignment.

She was halfway down the channel and no longer visible from the pier heads when she was joined, under way, by a dockyard lighter carrying three human-torpedoes.

The transfer of vehicles, from lighter to submarine, was accomplished without a hitch, and the torpedoes were carefully stowed in the *Scire*'s three torpedo cylinders — de la Penne's in the foredeck position, Marceglia's and Martellotta's in the two containers abaft the conning tower. Each of the three team-captains then gave his torpedo a meticulous going-over, checking for stowage security and for instrument response. It was close to midnight when they completed their work and joined Borghese on the darkened bridge.

"All set, skipper," they reported. "What happens next?"

Borghese gestured at the lighter, moving in alongside at slow speed. "She'll take you back to the pier," he said. "I'll see you at Leros ten days from now. You'll be flown from Brindisi to join me there, and that's when we'll wrap up the plan of attack. Meanwhile get lots of rest. You'll be needing it. Good-bye, for now."

As the team captains left, Borghese rang for slow ahead. The *Scire* moved cautiously out to sea, threading her way through minefields and then swinging south for the journey to the tip of Italy and beyond.

It was a voyage that held closely to schedule without undue excitement. At one point, off Taormina and the coast of Sicily, running surfaced in silver-bright moonlight, Borghese sighted a British submarine about one mile distant, idling across his path. The Italian Naval Command at Messina had warned him by radio a few hours earlier that such a submarine had been seen operating off nearby Cape dell 'Armi, following the track of an Axis convoy.

Borghese flashed word to Messina that he had the submarine in sight. Then he swung the *Scire* to face bows-on toward the enemy craft. He signalled it with his Aldis lamp, but received no intelligible reply. For long minutes then, each vessel held its position, unmoving. Finally Borghese turned the *Scire* back on course and put her under way again, heading once more toward the Aegean. As he did so, the enemy submarine also came to life. It moved onto a course parallel to the *Scire*'s and about a half-mile distant. For the next hour they proceeded in company, as though cruising in the same task force; then the British vessel silently swung away and turned back toward Sicily.

"Strange," murmured Borghese, watching from the bridge. "Strange things happen in wartime." He could think of no explanation for the incident. It was a mystery he never solved.

At dawn on the 9th, he entered the harbor of Port Lago on the island of Leros, guiding the *Scire* to station at the submarine pier, where sunlight streamed down across the tops of rocky ledges that rimmed the bay. It was a beautiful spot, but he had no time to enjoy the scenery. There was too much work to be done — messages to be sent and received, charts to be checked, photos to be studied — all in preparation for the upcoming attack.

Four days later, Borghese went by staff car to the far end of the island, to the Bay of Parteni, which earlier that year had been the departure point for the assault on Suda Bay. There he went aboard the camouflaged transport *Asmara* where the men from River Serchio, newly arrived, had been quartered for briefing. He assembled them in the ship's wardroom, grouping them before an enlarged chart of the Alexandria anchorage, complete with hydrographic and military details.

"We depart from Leros tomorrow morning," he told them. "As you certainly know by now, our target is Alexandria. Commander

Forza is in Athens, coordinating the necessary information traffic. Your orders are to sink the Valiant and the Queen Elizabeth and any other big prize within reach. The latest word from Athens is that they are sitting there waiting for you and are not expected to move.

"Your mission will be difficult," he went on, pointing out details on the chart. "The harbor is under heavy blackout. The channels of close approach are too shallow for effective submarine maneuvering. Our agents report that the harbor entrance is well guarded by minefields and other defenses. There's a thick minefield 20 miles northwest of the entrance. Closer in there's another field, covering about six miles. Then come long lines of detector cables. Then additional mines — and the usual net barriers, and patrol boats dropping depth charges.

"My plan is to approach the mainland at a depth of 200 feet, which should put us well below the outer field of mines. Our best time for attack will be on the 18th or 19th; there'll be no moon on those nights, and we can expect ideal weather conditions — calm, black, no wind.

"Shortly after dark, on completing our approach, I intend to release you at a position 1.3 miles from the lighthouse of Ras el Tin, at the outer tip of the harbor entrance. Then it will be up to you to make your way inside.

"Once you get in there, de la Penne will attack the Valiant — Marceglia the Queen Elizabeth — Martellotta, you look for the aircraft carrier Eagle, and if she's not there get yourself a big tanker. You can see on the chart, here, just where the target ships are moored.

"After you attack, if you get safely ashore, you are to pose as French seamen. There happen to be several French warships in the anchorage, and you can identify with them. I have all the necessary papers for you, along with some necessary pocket money.

"My orders, as usual, are to return to La Spezia as soon as you've left the Scire. However, we've assigned the submarine Zaffiro to cruise back and forth for two consecutive nights in an area 10 miles off Rosetta at the mouth of the Nile Delta. So if you get away successfully, your best bet is to head for Rosetta, steal a boat, and put to sea. The Zaffiro will be out there looking for you.

"Gentlemen, that's all for the moment. We can discuss any questions or details during the next few days on the way to Ras el Tin.

"Meanwhile you will be picked up here on the Asmara as soon as it's dark tonight, and brought directly to the Scire. We'll get under way shortly before sunrise. I'll see you aboard ship."

Back at Leros that night, Borghese sent a coded message to Forza at Athens: "Departing at dawn. Foresee cavities developing in lion's mouth."

In surface attack, (1) pilot aims self-exploding E-boat at target;

(2) after pilot ejects, explosive E-boat homes in on targeted ship.

Tenth Light Flotilla chart of attack on warships at Alexandria.

Battleship *HMS Queen Elizabeth*, knocked out in raid at Alexandria.

Chapter 18.
Clean Sweep

On the evening of December 18th, the shadows of twilight moved swiftly across Alexandria Harbor, casting a soft cloak over the big British ships that lay there at anchor.

Just before full darkness, at 1840 hours, at a point shortly beyond the west breakwater, the slender periscope of the *Scire* rose from the sea for a look around. It turned, paused, turned again slowly, and finally fastened its range on the Ras el Tin Lighthouse. Then it slipped down out of sight.

Below decks, Borghese stepped away from the periscope shaft to check his calculations. He reviewed his figures with satisfaction, and with justifiable pride in a job well done.

Actually, he had just completed on astonishing feat of navigation. Since leaving Leros on the 14th, he had brought the *Scire* more than 1700 miles, through one difficulty after another. A savage storm on the 16th had kept the submarine submerged for hours beyond its normal underwater running time, and meanwhile had put into motion strange new sea currents to contend with. There had been scant opportunity to get a daytime position-fix by sextant; most of the navigating had been done by compass, speed and mathematics, allowing for steering errors, compass deviation and the unpredictable variables of sea depth. For the last 16 hours of the voyage, the *Scire* had run submerged the whole time, navigating blindly, finally maneuvering beneath minefields to reach the coastal shallows.

And through all of this, the *Scire* had now come to rest at a point exactly 1.3 miles from Ras el Tin, bearing 356 degrees; Borghese had missed his designated arrival point by less then four feet.

For the next two hours, he held the *Scire* on the bottom, waiting for full darkness to cover the coast of Egypt. Then he surfaced to bridge-depth and climbed out alone on the conning tower to look around.

Conditions for the attack were as near perfect as he could hope for. The night was black and windless. The air soft. The sea was calm, its temperature moderately cool. The sky was clear, promising a night of serenity. In the distance, the light of Ras el Tin glimmered like a shaft of silver, marking the entrance to the harbor. Borghese nodded with satisfaction, and assembled the attack-teams for departure. The time was 8:47.

"Follow the orders of de la Penne," he told them. "He'll be in command — until you separate."

"And now for the usual kick for good luck?" said Marceglia.

"A special one for Bianchi this time," Borghese said. "His wife gave birth to a daughter today. Forza sent word from Athens an hour ago."

Bianchi stood grinning excitedly as the others pumped his hand. "That's good news in two ways," he said. "Now I know I'll survive."

"God be with you all," said Borghese. "Good hunting and a safe journey."

"Safe journey home," they told him.

De la Penne and Bianchi led the way, mounting their torpedo and moving off quickly into the blackness of the sea. Marceglia and Schergat followed within moments, then Martellotta and Marino.

With their departure, Borghese submerged to the bottom and held the *Scire* there for several minutes, tracking the faint and fading sounds of the torpedoes by hydrophone. Then he turned the submarine northward, moving out toward the open sea and the long course home.

As the *Scire* slipped away to the north, the Serchio teams astride their torpedoes moved cautiously southwest and then south, following the long, broad angle of the Ras el Tin breakwater. They proceeded in company for two hours, navigating without incident, crossing safely beneath the beam of the lighthouse.

Near the tip of the breakwater, de la Penne signaled the other pilots to halt. He beckoned them to close in, and spoke to them in half-whispered tones.

"Things have been going too easy," he pointed out. "We're running too far ahead of schedule. We'll take a break here — relax for a bit before going in."

The others murmured agreement and broke open their ration tins. De la Penne distributed small bottles of cognac. For the next half-hour or so, they stayed grouped in a circle on the dark and quiet sea, eating figs and raisin cakes, sipping their cognac, and glancing off occasionally toward the tall tower of the lighthouse that marked the end of the breakwater, scarcely 500 yards away.

At length, de la Penne gave the word to get under way again, and they submerged until only their heads were showing above water. In that way, they moved close to the edge of the net defenses that guarded the harbor entrance. There they could plainly hear the voices of men on the extreme end of the breakwater, conversing in the dark shadows just overhead. They could see one man moving about, passing close by, carrying a lighted oil-lamp. In the near foreground of the channel, a large motorboat cruised back and forth on slow patrol, running with near-silent motors, occasionally dropping random depth charges.

De la Penne studied the situation for several minutes, trying to plan how best to approach the nets and cut a passage through without being detected. Then, abruptly, the problem solved itself. To his astonished delight, two sets of red and green lights suddenly flashed on, outlining the bounds of the entrance channel. As he watched, scarcely believing his luck, the net barrier swung wide open. And churning in from the sea came three British destroyers, running in column formation, speeding in toward port to seek the harbor anchorage.

The ships passed so close that the Serchio men could hear the voices of seamen and the clanking of chains on deck. The onrushing bow of the lead destroyer nearly washed de la Penne from his torpedo. Instantly, then, the three pilots kicked their vehicles ahead to top speed and surged into the foaming wake of the enemy ships.

They rode the churning waters with only their heads above the surface. They plunged through the gap side by side, barely a foot apart, with de la Penne in the middle and Martellotta on his right. Behind them, the nets swung shut and the lights blinked out. One by one, they swung their torpedoes out of the wake of the warships and reduced speed to a slow drift. They were in darkness again, but this time it was the darkness of the inner harbor itself. And somewhere nearby were their targets. The teams quickly separated, each to pursue its own mission.

De la Penne knew where the *Valiant* should be. Air reconnaissance photos had shown it anchored at a mooring site that lay roughly northeast of his present position, bearing approximately 60 degrees. He checked his compass and set out in that direction, dropping the stern of his torpedo so that Bianchi was completely submerged. Only de la Penne's head rode above the surface of the water.

After several minutes, he sighted the dark outline of the big French battleship *Lorraine*, helplessly interned at Alexandria for the past 18 months. He took a bearing on the warship's bow, and moved off toward where the *Valiant* should be moored. He found her without difficulty, noting that she was surrounded by anti-torpedo netting which hung suspended from a ring of clanking buoys.

He paused, beginning to shiver with cold. Somewhere along the way he had ripped his diving suit, possibly upon leaving the *Scire*. Now the water, leaking, was giving him a wet chill. He signaled Bianchi to swim out ahead and lean his weight on the top strand of the barrier. As the netting sank down, de la Penne drove his torpedo over the top and came to rest on the other side, within 100 feet of the battleship. He glanced at his watch; it was 2:19. He submerged his vehicle to 15 feet below the surface and moved forward at dead-slow speed. Gently, the torpedo nudged against a barrier of steel. De la Penne reached out, and his groping hand came to rest on the *Valiant's* hull.

At precisely that instant, with success almost assured, the fate of the attack-mission swung abruptly toward disaster. The propeller of the human-torpedo became tangled in a steel cable and snarled to a halt. In a flash of dismay, de la Penne felt the vehicle lurch beneath him. It plunged to the bottom of the harbor, 55 feet down, carrying the two men with it and coming to rest at an angled position several yards away from the warship's keel. Almost simultaneously, Bianchi's breathing-gear collapsed, forcing him to flounder hurriedly to the surface.

Left alone, de la Penne worked desperately in the slime and the black water, trying to right the damage. He could feel the tangled cable on the torpedo's propeller and knew it would be impossible to free it by hand. Yet, somehow, he would have to move the weapon to a position directly under the *Valiant* or abandon the whole mission.

He surfaced to get his bearings. There was no sign of Bianchi. He dove to the torpedo again and began tugging it by muscle-power, edging it inch by inch toward the pulsing sound of the *Valiant*'s huge generators, repeating almost step by step the solo drama performed by Birindelli at Gibraltar more than a year earlier.

For 40 minutes, de la Penne pushed and hauled. Clouds of black mud made visibility impossible. Water seeped into his face mask; and he drank it to get rid of it. He tugged and pulled, sweating and panting, tortured by cramps, finally coming to the very edge of collapse. But always, minute by minute, the sounds from the *Valiant* grew stronger, beckoning him straight to his target.

At length, he straightened up for one last effort. And as he did, his head bumped the warship's keel. He was in perfect target position, directly under the midships section. He set the warhead's time fuse for a 6 a.m. explosion, then swam to the surface, concealing himself under the flare of the ship's bow. The cool night air quickly revived him and drove away his fatigue. He stripped off his breathing-gear and sank it, then began to swim away from the ship, moving slowly and cautiously in the shadows.

A shout from the battleship's deck brought him to an abrupt halt.

"You, down there! Stop or get shot!"

The glare of a searchlight pinned him in the water. A sudden burst of machine-gun fire cut across his path.

"Get back here! Quick now! We're coming down for you!"

De la Penne turned and swam back to the bow of the ship, where he climbed aboard a mooring buoy. To his astonishment, he found Bianchi there, huddled in the shadows.

"Emilio! What happened to you?"

"Lost my air," said Bianchi. "Somehow I got aboard this thing and then passed out. When I revived I kept quiet, so there'd be no alarm."

De la Penne chuckled softly. "It's a good thing I found you — before you blew up."

"Then you did it! You set the fuse!"

"That I did," said de la Penne. "She's ticking away down there right now. Ticking nicely. Our English friends are in for a big surprise."

Several minutes later, a motor launch from the ship took them aboard under armed guard and carried them ashore, to a barracks near the lighthouse. There, they were stripped of their papers and subjected to sharp interrogation, but each refused to answer questions. A clock on the barracks wall stood at 4 a.m. when the English finally broke off the session and transported them back to the *Valiant*. And this time they were brought before the warship's commanding officer, Captain Charles E. Morgan.

"We assume you have placed a time bomb into a position to blow up the ship," he said to them. "I want to know where it is and when it will go off."

No answer.

"Very well, then," Morgan went on. "There's one sure way to make you talk. You'll be taken to a cell below decks and chained near an ammunition magazine. That's where you'll wait for the explosion. We'll see how long you remain silent."

Deep in the bowels of the ship, de la Penne and Bianchi were put in chains and given cigarettes and rations of rum. Two pale and nervous guards stayed with them, ready to rush the word to Morgan as soon as the details of the time bomb were disclosed. But the prisoners remained silent, sipping their rum, marking the slow but steady passage of time.

Finally, at 5:50, de la Penne broke the silence and asked to be taken to Captain Morgan immediately. They faced each other on the quarterdeck.

"Sir," said de la Penne, "in just a few minutes your ship will blow up. It's too late for you to prevent it. I'm here to suggest that you still have time to get your men to safety."

Morgan stared at him coldly. "How much time?"

"About 10 minutes," said de la Penne. "No more."

"For the last time, where is the bomb?"

"I refuse to answer."

"Guard!" Morgan shouted. "Take the prisoner back below. Lock him up!"

As he was hustled back below decks, de la Penne heard the ship's loudspeakers crackle into life. "Now hear this! All hands abandon ship! Abandon ship!"

The door of his cell banged shut behind him. He began to pray.

Meanwhile, through the dark hours of early morning, Marceglia and Schergat had been having a much easier time with their target, the *Queen Elizabeth.*

Photo reconnaissance had shown the big ship to be moored fairly close to shore. Marceglia therefore set out on a course that would parallel the waterfront and would take advantage of the lights on land to silhouette the anchored ships as he passed by.

It seemed to him that he had scarcely begun his search before he sighted the massive bulk of his target, the *Queen Elizabeth,* outlined against the shore lights and riding at anchor some 450 yards away. He closed in, dropping the stern of his torpedo and putting Schergat below the surface. He circled the outer edge of an anti-torpedo net, moved again toward his target, and finally came to a halt in the shadow of the ship's bow. Looking up, he could see the figure of a man on deck-watch, quiety smoking a cigarette.

Marceglia took a bearing on the ship's funnel, then submerged to a position directly under the *Elizabeth*'s keel. From there on, the operation proceeded exactly as it had been carried out during dozens of rehearsals at La Spezia and River Serchio. The attack-team located a stabilizer fin and attached a clamp and sling-line. Then, a clamp to the fin on the far side of the hull. Then, back to the central point of the line. There they attached the warhead, rigging it to hang about six feet below the ship's bottom. Marceglia glanced at his watch and activated the three-hour fuse. It was 3:15 a.m.

As soon as they got astride their torpedo for a getaway, Schergat made urgent signals to surface in a hurry. He was suffering from painful cramps, brought on by prolonged use of his oxygen gear. As quickly as he could, Marceglia brought the vehicle to the surface. They broached with a rush of air bubbles that momentarily aroused the attention of the *Elizabeth*'s afterdeck watch. A searchlight flashed on, swept across their heads, and then switched off again. All was dark and quiet once more as they set out for shore, leaving small fused fire-bombs behind them.

At 4:30 a.m., they swam ashore near an Egyptian slaughterhouse, close to the edge of a narrow, oily beach. There they buried their underwater gear and set out on foot for the heart of the city, intent on finding the railroad station and booking train passage for Rosetta.

The team of Martellotta and Marino, meanwhile, had been conducting somewhat of a solo harbor cruise in their search for a worthwhile target.

As they emerged on the inward side of the entrance barrier, Martellotta first followed a course of 120 degrees and then swung to 40 degrees, to pass between an inner breakwater and the dockside piers. The water was black and quiet, and the shore was well lighted. He identified, and cruised past, the French warship *Lorraine*. Farther ahead, he could make out the *Valiant* and the *Queen Elizabeth*. He set a course to pass between them and then to steer northeast in search of *HMS Eagle*, unaware that the aircraft carrier had departed that evening for Suez and the Indian Ocean. When he arrived at the carrier's anchorage and found it empty, he took off toward the nearest outlined warship. This, however, turned out to be only a light cruiser, and he started to pass her by in search of bigger game. As he did so, a sentry aboard the cruiser switched on a pocket flashlight, probing its beam at Martellotta's head. He lay still in the water for what seemed like endless minutes. Then the light snapped off, leaving him in darkness.

He raised his head again, and made out a group of tankers, moored some distance away near the waterfront piers. By now, both he and Marino were suffering from the strain of the operation. Their heads were aching, their stomachs were cramped. Martellotta began to vomit, and could no longer keep his mask in place. Angrily, he tore off his mouthpiece and threw it away, then moved the torpedo ahead again on the surface.

There were several tankers to choose from. Martellotta looked them over, one by one, cruising warily from ship to ship. Finally he settled on the biggest of the group. She was the *Sagona*, a 16,000-ton vessel, apparently fully loaded. He signaled to Marino, who dove down beneath the hull and easily attached the fused warhead. The time was 2:15 a.m.

As they were preparing to leave, the destroyer *HMS Jervis* pulled up to the *Sagona*'s far side and made ready to take on fuel. The two men congratulated each other with a handshake; this would be a long operation. "Let's hope she stays here another three hours," Marino whispered. "That will settle her hash." With that, they cruised away toward shore, leaving timed fire-bombs in their wake.

One hour later, while walking away from the harbor zone, they were arrested by Egyptian customs guards and turned over to a squad of British Marines.

It took nearly two hours for Egyptian and British officials to straighten out the red tape as to which government should have custody of the prisoners. During all that time, Martellotta and Marino were held in a waterfront police office and questioned by officers of both sides. Finally, the Egyptians conceded priority to the British, and a Royal Navy Commander took over the inquiry. He stripped them of all their belongings, including Martellotta's waterproof wristwatch, which was placed face upward on the Commander's desk.

"Now then," the officer told them, "I have sent for a car. When it arrives, we'll take you to Naval Headquarters at Ras el Tin. You are prisoners of war, of course. You will be sent to Cairo and then to Palestine. Meanwhile, we shall interrogate you thoroughly. You may smoke cigarettes and drink coffee while we wait for the car."

Martellotta stared fixedly at the upturned dial of his watch. It was 5:54. The seconds ticked on. The Commander studied a sheaf of papers in his hand. He raised his head. "First I should like to ask you — "

The watch ticked to 5:55. At that instant, a violent explosion jarred the whole building and boomed across the harbor. Bursts of flame reflected through the windows. Sirens screamed. Martellotta and Marino grinned at each other; there went the *Sagona*, and probably *Jervis* as well.

Moments later, at 6:04, another tremendous explosion rocked the harbor; there went the *Valiant*.

At 6:15, the *Queen Elizabeth* blew up.

Some miles away, relaxing on a passenger bench at the Alexandria railroad station, Marceglia and Schergat heard the three explosions and silently shook hands. They were destined to be caught and arrested the next day while trying to cash a five-pound note at Rosetta; but even had they known, that fact was not important. They had carried out their mission. Nothing else mattered.

Meanwhile aboard the *Valiant*, the explosion beneath that ship had bucked the vessel out of the water and slammed it back with a sharp list to port. De la Penne, alone in his cell, was hurled against a bulkhead and battered by falling chains. Sea water poured in through an open porthole. Lights went out and the hold filled with smoke. The hull of the vessel hit bottom, and the ship continued to list. Bianchi was gone, somewhere. De la Penne hastily fought his way up ladders and crawled through a hatchway to the open deck. The harbor was a shambles of confusion. In the near distance, he saw a tanker ablaze. He turned and ran aft, to come face to face with Captain Morgan.

"Where's my diver!" de la Penne yelled. "Where's Bianchi!"

Morgan was too busy shouting orders to pay him any attention. De la Penne hurried to the stern. He stood there staring at the *Queen Elizabeth*, some 500 yards away. A few seconds passed. Then the *Elizabeth* too went up with a thundering roar. She rose several inches out of the water and then plunged back, listing to starboard. Admiral Cunningham, standing on his flagship's fantail, was blown three feet into the air and came down on his heels. Oil, water and debris from the explosion showered down across the harbor and spattered the deck of the *Valiant*. De la Penne closed his eyes in a brief gesture of gratitude; the Serchio mission was over.

Moments later, he made his way to the officers' wardroom, and there he found Bianchi, drinking coffee while confusion swirled around him.

They sat together and exchanged tight-lipped smiles of satisfaction.

"Clean sweep," said de la Penne. "Three for three."

"With a bonus of one destroyer," said Bianchi. "She was alongside the tanker."

"Good. I didn't know about that. Where were you when it happened?"

"In here," said Bianchi. "They were questioning me again. Have some coffee. They're going to lock us up at Ras el Tin for a while. Then we'll visit Cairo and go on to Palestine."

"Naturally," said de la Penne. "And I'll bet we'll all be together for Christmas."

For the men from River Serchio, the score was excellent. At the small cost of six men taken prisoner, they had sunk one of the Royal Navy's largest tankers, badly damaged a destroyer, and put two battleships out of commission. Most important, the *Valiant* and the *Queen Elizabeth*, with their keels resting on the bottom of the harbor, would be out of action for months to come, the *Valiant* with internal damages and an 80-foot gash in her side, the *Elizabeth* with three boiler compartments demolished and her hull ripped wide open. Suddenly the British were without battleships in the Mediterranean. Overnight, the sea had become an Axis lake. And the Italian Navy held dominating power.

Not until four months later did Winston Churchill feel it wise to reveal to the people of Britain the extent and significance of their Mediterranean losses. Then on April 23, 1942, he finally did so before a secret session of the House of Commons. In reporting on setbacks suffered by the Royal Navy, he concluded with bitterness:

"A further sinister stroke was to come.

"On the early morning of December 19, half a dozen Italians in unusual diving suits were captured floundering about in the harbor of Alexandria. Extreme precautions have been taken for some time past against the varieties of human-torpedo or one-man submarine entering our harbors. Not only are nets and other obstructions used but underwater charges are exploded at frequent irregular intervals in the fairway.

"None the less, these men had penetrated the harbor. Four hours later, explosions occurred in the bottoms of the 'Valiant' and the 'Queen Elizabeth', produced by limpet bombs fixed with extraordinary courage and ingenuity, the effect of which was to blow large holes in the bottoms of both ships and to flood several compartments, thus putting them out of action for many months.

"One ship will soon be ready again. The other is still in the floating dock at Alexandria, a constant target for enemy air attack. Thus we no longer had any battle squadron in the Mediterranean. 'Barham' had gone, and now the 'Valiant' and 'Queen Elizabeth' were completely out of action.

"Both of these ships floated on an even keel. They looked all right from the air. The enemy were for some time unaware of the success of their attack, and it is only now that I feel it possible to make this disclosure to the House, even in the strictness of a Secret Session.

"The Italian fleet still contains four or five battleships, several times repaired, of the new 'Littorio' or of the modernized class. The sea defense of the Nile Valley had to be confided to our submarine and destroyer flotillas, with a few cruisers, and of course to shore-based Air Forces.

"For this reason, it was necessary to transfer a part of our shore-based torpedo-carrying aircraft from the south and east coasts of England, where they were soon to be needed, to the North African shore...."

Meanwhile Borghese had arrived back at La Spezia just 10 days after the victory at Alexandria, bringing the *Scire* safely home from an operational voyage of 3500 miles. Awaiting him were congratulatory messages from Supermarina and a personal directive from King Victor Emmanuel, awarding him the decoration of the Military Order of Savoy. The citation read:

"Commanding Officer of a submarine detailed to the Tenth Light Flotilla for special assault craft operation, he had already successfully carried out three daring and difficult undertakings. He studied and prepared, with great technical competence and shrewdness, the plan of a fourth operation, for forcing a further enemy base. He took his submarine close in to the heavily fortified harbor, facing with cool determination the risks incurred from the defense measures and vigilance of the enemy, in order to put the assault craft in the best possible position for forcing the enemy base. He then landed the assault craft in an action which achieved a brilliant success, leading as it did to the infliction of serious damage upon two enemy battleships."

It was a gratifying honor, of course. But it could scarcely compensate for the despair that mounted in Borghese's heart as he waited in vain through the following weeks for some sign that the great victory at Alexandria would be properly exploited. No such sign ever developed.

This he could not understand. As he (correctly) saw the situation, neither the *Valiant* nor the *Queen Elizabeth* would ever again be a contributing factor to the outcome of the war. Italy was now the supreme naval power in the Mediterranean. It would be many months before sufficient reserve strength from Britain or untapped power from the United States could be assembled to challenge that superiority.

Meanwhile the way was wide open for an Axis assault against Malta. An invasion force, backed by Italian battleships, would in all certainty be able to crush the fortress island and eliminate it as a strategic stronghold. With this done, the path would be cleared for pouring supplies and troops into North Africa, overrunning the Allies in Egypt, and grabbing the valuable resources of the Middle East. In short, total victory lay within reach.

Churchill recognized the danger, and warned his countrymen. Admiral Weichold, German liaison officer with Supermarina, recognized the opportunity and criticized the German High Command for its "underestimation of sea power and the importance of the Mediterranean." And Borghese fretted helplessly, blaming both the German High Command and the Italian General Staff for failure to act.

Idled at La Spezia, he waited with fading hope for orders that would send the Tenth Light back to sea. But when the orders finally came, they sent the Flotilla in the wrong direction — to the Crimea, by land.

Chapter 19.
Change of Tactics

While the Mediterranean lay vulnerable, the German High Command in the spring of 1942 stubbornly chose to reach out instead toward the Caspian Sea and the Caucasus Mountains. Germany's drive to win these objectives had stalled at Sebastopol and Balaclava in the Crimean Peninsula. Russian defenders, under siege in those ancient Black Sea ports, were being pounded on three sides by German land forces but were constantly being revitalized from the fourth side by troops and supplies that poured in from the sea. And Germany, impressed by the operations of the Tenth Light Flotilla, called upon the Italian Navy to cut off the Soviet sea routes and to help choke the two fortress-cities into submission.

Supermarina responded by assigning a small force to go to the Black Sea and test the situation, using four-man CB submarines and MTSM torpedo-motorboats. The immediate results were excellent. The CB units sank two Russian submarines, while one of the motorboats engaged and sank a cruiser.

On the strength of this, the Tenth Light Flotilla was ordered to put together an expeditionary force of 48 men, five torpedo-motorboats and five E-boats, to be moved to the Crimea by railroad and to enter the battle as quickly as possible. The force had its own tractors, trucks, repair facilities and communication equipment. It carried enough fuel, ammunition, spare parts and food rations to sustain itself for months to come. It was named the "Moccagatta Column." Because of the specialized demands of the mission, which involved surface attacks only, none of Borghese's human-torpedo teams were included.

On May 19, then, after an overland journey of two weeks, the 40 vehicles of the column detrained at Simferopol, in the heart of the Crimea, and took to the mountainous highways. Two days later they rolled into Yalta on the southeast coast, then rumbled on to the little southern port of Foros, where the column would be headquartered.

There were many problems to overcome. For the time being, the entire expedition was encamped in the open, under the trees. Now, living quarters and administrative offices had to be built, and roadways laid out. Launching facilities had to be constructed. Meanwhile, the work was constantly being interrupted by air attacks, with Soviet planes bombing and strafing against a feeble anti-aircraft defense of only two 20-millimeter guns.

Nevertheless, just 13 days after arrival the Tenth Light began operations at sea. And for the next month, by night and by day, they struck blow after blow against Russian ships attempting to ferry supplies to the defenders of Balaclava and Sebastopol.

On June 6, the River Serchio men with their torpedo-motorboats joined German Stormboats in attacking and scattering a Russian convoy. On June 10, they engaged the Russian cruiser *Tashkent*. The following day they attacked a Russian torpedo-boat. Two days later, a lone MTSM intercepted a big Russian supply ship of 13,000 tons, escorted by a torpedo-boat and two light auxiliaries and bound for Sebastopol with a full cargo of ammunition. The MTSM made its run on the big Russian, scored a direct hit with a torpedo and drove the flaming ship ashore, where it was left to be finished off by air attack.

On another occasion, in a sea assault on Fort Gorki, near Sebastopol, eight Serchio men armed themselves with hand grenades and automatic rifles and stormed ashore at the rear of the fort while the Germans were attacking by land. As the fort collapsed, the Italian "infantry-sailors" collared 80 Russian prisoners.

So it went. And the flow of supplies to the besieged cities rapidly dwindled to a small, ineffective trickle.

On the 29th of June, the German offensive schedule called for the storming of Balaclava by Romanian troops in a landing-attack from the sea. On that day, therefore, the five MTSMs joined German units in carrying out a mock diversionary landing south of the city, staging a thunderous display of gunfire and explosions that utterly confused the Russian defense forces. Two days later, as the Romanians overran the city with their bayonets, the Serchio men in their motorboats sped into the harbor to close the channels against seaborne relief and to prevent the Russian defenders from escaping. Balaclava fell; and the Romanian Command, celebrating in the ruins, feted the Serchio men with champagne and onions.

Six days later, the battered fortress of Sebastopol also fell. German troops, storming in to secure the city, were followed closely by men of the Tenth Light, who found the devastation appalling. As one Flotilla journal described it:

"The place was in utter ruins. A cruiser and a destroyer had sunk in the harbor. All docks and workshops had been shattered. Corpses were floating in the water and lying in the streets under clouds of flies. In the courtyard, wounded Russian civilians were crouching on the steps or stretched on the ground, silently waiting for death. No one uttered a cry or a groan. Some of the living were still lying among the dead bodies which had not yet been removed. Nothing but dust, heat, flies, dead and yet more dead. Passers-by were avoiding the neighborhood of a dug-up mine as they walked, stepping over corpses. So it went on...."

In the wake of Sebastopol, the men of the Tenth Light remained with the German forces for another eight months. But now that the prime objective of their mission had been achieved, there was little else to accomplish or to keep them busy.

They moved in August from Foros to Theodosia. They moved again, to Yalta, to Melitopol, and finally to Mariupol on the Sea of Azov, where they stayed idle for many weeks, waiting for the Germans to advance to the Caspian Sea.

But then came winter, and with it came a turn in the tide of war; bulwarked by supplies from the United States, the Russians abandoned their strategy of scorched-earth defense and went on the offensive. It soon became apparent that the Germans were not going to reach the Caspian; they were, in fact, beginning to withdraw in the opposite direction.

And so, in January, the men of the Moccagatta Column were ordered by Supermarina to pack their gear for the long journey home from Mariupol. They had achieved what they'd set out to achieve; there was no point in remaining. It was now time to pack up, to sail across to Constanta on the coast of Romania, and then head home for Italy.

Two months later, the Moccagatta Column arrived back at La Spezia, as fully equipped as when it had left. Through travels and battles, the 10-month operation had been carried out without a loss.

In the meantime, while the Moccagatta Column had been busy at the Russian Front, Prince Borghese had arrived at an abrupt change of direction in his activies with the Tenth Light. He received orders relieving him from command of the *Scire* and assigning him to duties that struck him at first as being highly nebulous and non-constructive. His reaction was to request a meeting with the Naval Ministry at Rome and to ask that the orders be reconsidered. The meeting was arranged, and he drove to Rome from La Spezia to sit with a Ministry board and present his arguments.

"If it's at all possible, I prefer to stay with the Scire," he said flatly. "The record shows that we are an excellent operational unit. We have accomplished every mission. What purpose can be served by breaking up a winning team?"

He met with no encouragement. "The fact that you're a winning team is one of the reasons for this action," they told him. "It's time we developed more winners."

"But these orders." said Borghese, "state that upon leaving the Scire I am to concentrate upon developing and broadening the attack potential of the underwater division. I have already been doing that, and with good success. The orders futher indicate that I am to travel abroad in the near future with a view to expanding the division's capabilities. How do these responsibilities relate? And how would they conflict with my role if I continued as skipper of the Scire?"

"Commander Borghese," came the reply, "as we said, we need more winners. You have carried out five operations in command of the Scire — four to Gibraltar and one to Alexandria. Your part in each operation has been a complete success.

"You have shown us how best to use the submarine in this type of service. Your suggestions for technical improvement have resulted in an assault potential far beyond anything we had hoped for. We are grateful. And when you comprehend the scope of action involved in your new orders, you will understand what we mean. The orders reflect our appreciation, our trust and our confidence in you.

"In the meantime, you have trained the crew of the Scire to the ultimate level of skill and efficiency. You have analyzed the enemy harbor defenses and have written the answers to all problems of navigation and attack-approach for any objective in the Mediterranean.

"Now, Commander, it's time for other officers to learn the trade. We need them to replace you. And we need you for something much bigger than anything you've ever attempted."

"I'm honored," said Borghese. "But you're talking of something more important than Alexandria?"

"Much more important. But before we get into that, let's discuss the matter of your going abroad. Then it will begin to come clear."

Borghese nodded. "Please go on."

"Very well. When we speak of further developing the attack potential of your underwater division, we don't mean that you'll be working at La Spezia or River Serchio. For you, that's all in the past.

"You will be going first to Berlin. This will be an exchange of favors, so to speak. The Germans are working hard to set up a Tenth Light organization of their own. Their training base is on the shore of a large lake in Brandenburg. They have asked for assistance — specifically for you.

"We've invited them to send a group of selected officers and seamen to Italy to attend the regular training courses of the Tenth. These men will then return to Brandenburg as instructors. But meanwhile, we have agreed to a request from Berlin that you pay a visit to Brandenburg and get their program started on the right course."

"And what does Italy get in this exchange of favors?" said Borghese.

The answer was short and direct. "Secrets pertaining to naval sabotage, Commander. The Germans are masters in that field. We need to share this knowledge. We also need certain information they have acquired through their submarine warfare in the Atlantic and off the coast of North America."

"I see." Borghese leaned forward to accept a cigar from one of his host officers. "And then? After Berlin?"

"And then, Commander, you will go to Paris for a meeting with Admiral Doenitz — on a matter that we'll discuss with you shortly. If that meeting is successful, as we expect it to be, you will visit our Atlantic Submarine Base at Bordeaux for a special appraisal of our ocean-going submarines. After that, you will go to Madrid and Lisbon, where your contacts again will be certain experts in naval sabotage.

"Now do you begin to understand, Commander Borghese? Do you see why the command of the Scire is so unimportant when compared to our long-range program for you? Your success with the Scire has been outstanding. Now we have much bigger plans, involving a much bigger submarine."

Borghese stared at them without speaking, as the implications became clear. "And the target? It's America?"

Heads nodded. "The target will be New York, Commander. For obvious reasons, there's no hint of such a plan in your orders. However, we knew you would come to Rome and we could tell you in person. From this moment on, the project is yours. Now we'd like to hear your comments."

Borghese let out his breath in a long sigh of satisfaction. "I've been dreaming about this for months, but never mentioned it to anybody. I never imagined you'd support it. As a matter of fact, I have some very definite suggestions...."

Several weeks later, on April 2, Borghese took part in his last formal ceremony as Commanding Officer of the *Scire.*. The occasion was the awarding of decorations for gallantry. With the permission of the Ministry, he had advised his crew that any man aboard could request and receive a transfer from the *Scire* to some less dangerous billet, as a reward for courageous and loyal service. But the entire ship's company had elected to stay with the submarine, and now stood drawn up in ranks awaiting honors.

Full-dressed for the occasion, the *Scire* lay moored at Veleria Pier in La Spezia, flanked by two other submarines. On Borghese's left was the U-81, commanded by Lieutenant Gugenberger, whose men had sunk the aircraft carrier *Ark Royal*. On *Scire*'s other flank rode the U-331, commanded by Lieutenant Von Tiesenhausen, whose men had sunk the *Barham*.

It was a brilliant ceremony, bright with color and flair. As bugles sounded, the men stiffened to attention. Then, reading the citations in the name of the King, the Duke of Aosta awarded the medals to each man by name. The men of the *Scire* received four apiece.

Upon leaving the *Scire*, Borghese carried with him the echoes of an ear-shattering farewell cheer from the crew and a framed photograph of the ship, autographed by every man aboard.

He was never to see the submarine again. Four months later, on her first mission after Borghese gave up command, she was ordered to Leros to prepare for an attack on British shipping in the Palestinian port of Haifa. She never returned.

The targets looked promising. The crushing advance of Axis troops across North Africa to El Alamein had alarmed the British into dispersing ships that were normally kept at Alexandria. Some were sent through the Suez Canal to the Red Sea, safely beyond reach of Italian Navy units. But at the beginning of August, German air reconnaissance photos of the harbor at Haifa disclosed that the British had anchored a small fleet in that port — a fleet consisting of two cruisers, three destroyers, eight cargo ships and transports, four tankers, five patrol boats, two torpedo-boats and two submarines.

Haifa immediately became a prime target for assault. The *Scire*, with a crew of 50 men aboard, was ordered to leave Leros on August 6 with 10 River Serchio frogmen and to release them off the coast of Palestine on the night of August 10. Her orders were to head back to Leros on the 11th, with whatever survivors she had managed to take aboard.

Lieutenant Commander Max Candiani, head of plans and operations at River Serchio, was sent to Rhodes to direct and coordinate the mission. In his opinion, all portents were favorable. Calm weather was forecast, with a light, protective mist after dark. The men were all experienced hands at this sort of thing. And Haifa was known to have only secondary harbor defenses at best. On the surface, everything seemed to favor a successful attack. Spirits were high aboard the *Scire* as she sailed out of Leros on the 6th.

Three nights later, the submarine acknowledged a routine situation report from Rhodes and confirmed her attack schedule for the night of the 10th. Then she began her slow approach to the ancient seaport-city.

Entries in Candiani's diary picked up the story from there:

14 August — Nothing yet heard from the Scire. The delay may be due to the desire of the submarine, with enemy units in the zone, not to incur the risk of radio messages being overheard.

— 1700 hours. Still no news. Sent message to the Scire requesting information.

— 2200 hours. No reply from submarine.

15 August — 0800 hours. Still no news.. Requested Aegean Air Force to carry out special reconnaissance over Haifa.

— 1500 hours. Aircraft, which flew within sight of Haifa, returned without information.

— 1800 hours. Requested Tenth German Group to carry out air reconnaissance over Haifa, which I hope will give me evidence as to the fate of Scire.

16 August — Still no news of the Scire.

17 August — 0500 hours. A German J-86 has left Crete in attempt at Haifa reconnaissance.

— 0800 hours. Aircraft succeeded in photographing harbor from 9000 meters and will bring print to Rhodes.

— 2200 hours. Photograph obtained and examined. No vessel damaged and no trace of forcing of harbor. I infer that the Scire, of which there is still no news whatever, never reached the stage of dropping the operators.

It had all been a waste. On the night of the 10th, while moving in for the attack-approach, the *Scire* had been spotted and depth-charged by the British torpedo-boat *Islay*. The submarine went down with all hands. In death, she was awarded the Gold Medal for Gallantry.

Borghese heard the news later that month, on his return from Paris to La Spezia. His reaction was to seclude himself in his quarters, sitting late into the night with a bottle of wine, re-reading the logs of his submarine voyages and remembering with affection the men who had served for so many months under his command.

He had hoped to bring them all together again, to sail with them across the Atlantic. Now, more than ever, he was determined to reach New York.

Chapter 20.
Gibraltar, in
Residence

W hile the Moccagatta Column had been fighting Russians in the Crimea, Borghese and other leaders of the Tenth Light had initiated a project designed to develop new tactics for the sinking of ships at Gibraltar.

What bothered the River Serchio tacticians the most were the logistical problems involved in reaching their distant targets. Each blow at Gibraltar in the past had required a long submarine voyage, air and land transportation of the attack-teams, the shipping of supplies and weapons, arrangements for rendezvous, an approach by submarine, and finally the task of smuggling the survivors back to Italy without jostling the delicate neutrality balance of the Spanish Government.

In spite of all these handicaps, the system had worked fairly well. Out of 24 operators who had been dropped off by submarine at Gibraltar's anchorage, 22 had made it safely back to River Serchio. The only ones lost had been Birindelli and Paccagnini, who had been taken prisoner in the raid of October 1940.

Still, it was a cumbersome system. And one of its potentially dangerous features was that the smuggling of men and supplies in and out of Spain, usually by way of the Pyrenees Mountains, depended for success almost entirely on the performace of one man — a swashbuckling Italian secret agent named Pepo Martini, who had taken up permanent residence in Spain. So far, Pepo had carried out every task assigned to him; but there was always the danger of his being discovered and put out of action. Now, Rome decided, it was time to enlist his help in establishing a permanent attack-base on Spanish soil, as close to Gibraltar as possible.

Pepo had his share of detractors in Supermarina, men who felt he could not be trusted and might easily be bought out by the enemy. But he had strong support where it counted most, in the person of Italy's Director of Naval Intelligence, Admiral Franco Maugeri.

"Pepo," Maugeri once remarked, "is as rascally, ruthless, shrewd and charming a scoundrel as ever walked the earth. But he knows everybody and he gets things done.

"He is the typical Hollywood idea of the undercover agent — young, handsome, dashing, daring, quick-witted, resourceful. Women, young and old, are drawn to him like dogs to a bone. And Pepo, though he loves his wife, is not at all averse to being the bone."

Pepo had been a sergeant in the Italian Army during the Spanish Civil War. He had fallen in love with Spain and with a beautiful, red-haired Spanish senorita, whose brother was a high official in Franco's Foreign Office. When the Civil War ended, Pepo married the senorita and took her to live in San Sebastian, near the French border.

There Pepo achieved political power, partly through his own bold tactics and partly through his wife's influence in Madrid. He became a secretary of one of Spain's strong pro-Fascist groups. He enjoyed a position of force in local politics, developed connections in high circles throughout Spain's major cities, and otherwise occupied himself by running a profitable smuggling business of the side. When Italy entered the war in 1940, Pepo offered Rome his services and his talents, which included linguistic perfection in Spanish and French. He was a valuable operator.

In Maugeri's opinion, Pepo wanted a piece of the war-action "not out of any great feeling of patriotism or sense of loyalty, but simply because he loves adventure and hopes to advance himself politically." Maugeri never fully trusted Pepo, but liked and admired him. And he saw in Pepo the ideal man to place in charge of all smuggling operations between the Pyrenees and Algeciras.

"My judgement was more than justified," Maugeri later recalled. "Working with Pepo, we never lost a man or a piece of equipment."

Thus it was to Pepo Martini that Supermarina appealed for help in the spring of 1942 when the decision was made to establish a base for the Tenth Light Flotilla right at Gibraltar's doorstep. Convoy ships for the United States were beginning to arrive in quantity. The numbers of potential targets at anchor in the Bay of Algeciras were growing almost daily. And since Pepo had been so successful at smuggling men out of Spain, why not use him to smuggle men and supplies into a permanent attack-base at Algeciras and thus do away with the long submarine voyages? Pepo was agreeable to the idea; but first, where was the base?

The answer to that problem came from a talented Italian engineer named Antonio Ramognino, who had volunteered for Navy duty with the Tenth Light. He had earlier spent considerable time in the vicinity of Algeciras, and had recently married a charming Spanish lady, Signora Conchita.

"How would it be," he suggested to the Serchio planners, "if I take Conchita to Algeciras for our honeymoon? And suppose we let it be known that she's in poor health and needs a lot of sea air and sunbathing.

"I happen to know of a bungalow for rent that would be just right for her. It's called the Villa Carmela. It's on a small rise that slopes to a private beach at Maiorga Point near La Linea. A great many ships from the convoys anchor there after coming through the Straits — some of them 2,000 yards offshore, others within 600 yards of the beach. Every move they make can be seen from the Villa."

"Very good, Antonio," they told him. "And is Signora Conchita willing to receive occasional guests?"

Ramognino nodded. "She assures me that she is quite willing. In fact, she says it will help her recover to entertain her good friends from Italy."

"And you do not anticipate a speedy recovery, of course."

"Certainly not. Conchita says it may be months before she's feeling like herself again. We would be at Algeciras for a long time."

Without further delay, Ramognino and his wife flew to Spain as a honeymooning couple and soon traveled south to Algeciras, where they signed a lease for Villa Carmela. Because of the signora's poor health and her need for sunlight, they got permission from the owner to install a new window on the side of the bungalow that faced out across Algeciras Bay and Gibraltar Harbor, offering a sweeping view of the sea. The signora then hung a cage of green parakeets just outside the window and could be seen there several times a day, taking care of her birds.

When they were settled in, Pepo Martini became a frequent visitor at the bungalow. Then he went to the north of Spain on a business trip.

Shortly after that, in July 1942, a group of 12 frogmen left River Serchio, each carrying three limpet mines in his gear. Six of them went to the Italian Navy's Atlantic Submarine Base at Bordeaux. From there, three of them entered Spain in the false bottom of a truck driven by one of Pepo's friends, and the other three were escorted across the Pyrenees on foot. Meanwhile, the remaining six of the original group arrived in Barcelona as deckhands aboard an Italian freighter. They immediately deserted their ship and made contact with another of Pepo's agents.

Eventually all 12 of the frogmen were assembled in Madrid, where cars were waiting to drive them to Cadiz as "crew replacements" assigned to the tanker *Fulgor*. From there, traveling one or two at a time, it was an easy step to reach Algeciras and the Villa Carmela. And on the morning of July 13, staring out past the parakeet cage, they chose their targets for attack.

That night, hidden by darkness, the frogmen left silently from Villa Carmela and headed for the beach. They made their way across a flower garden and down the grassy slope, keeping close to the shadows of a sheltering wall. The beach was silent and empty. Lights from the convoy ships at anchor flickered across the dark water. The frogmen checked each other's blackened faces, donned hairnets interlaced with seaweed camouflage, adjusted their fins, and then waded quietly into the water to begin the swim to their targets.

British patrolboats occasionally circled by. Now and then a searchlight from a ship's bridge would flick on and stab at the water, then flick off again. The frogmen paired off into teams and went their slow and separate ways in the darkness. They swam easily and quietly, from time to time pausing to tread water so that the tops of their heads looked like floating seaweed. One by one, the teams reached their targets and dove down to attach their limpet mines.

It was 3:20 in the morning when the first two frogmen to return waded ashore and walked up the beach toward the Villa. Two others followed shortly, emerging from the water onto a strip of sand close to the Ramognino's front lawn. A fifth man returned to shore some distance away at La Linea Bridge and followed the beach road to the bungalow. The seven remaining frogmen waded out of the sea at a point that was being guarded that night by Spanish police. The swimmers were arrested and questioned, but were promptly released in custody of one of Pepo's agents.

By dawn, all 12 frogmen were back together again at Villa Carmela, where Signora Conchita was awaiting them with coffee, cognac, cigarettes and a warm breakfast. Pepo's drivers arrived shortly to take them back to Cadiz and the *Fulgor*.

With daylight came proof of the value of the Villa as an advanced base. Out in the harbor, violent explosions suddenly rocked four British merchant ships — the *Meta*, the *Shuma*, the *Empire Snipe* and the *Baron Douglas*. All four had to be run ashore with frantic speed to prevent them from sinking. Each suffered heavily, in hull damage and cargo loss.

A similar operation, but on a much smaller scale, was launched from the Villa Carmela two months later. And again, the result was a loss for the British.

On this occasion, only two frogmen were despatched from River Serchio and, with Pepo's help, were smuggled into Spain. They arrived in Barcelona as deckhands aboard the Italian freighter *Mario Croce*, and promptly jumped ship to meet with one of Pepo's waterfront agents. They were taken to Algeciras, where they joined three of the original Carmela group who had stayed behind after the July attack.

All five men, disguised as merchant seamen, were successfully spirited through town and out to Ramognino's bungalow, where Signora Conchita again performed the duties of a gracious hostess.

By darkfall on the 14th, after hours of studying convoy ships from the bungalow window, the plans for attack had been completed, but the proposed scope of the attack itself had been sharply curtailed. There were good reasons for this. The British, made wary by the July operation, had altered their convoy anchorage pattern, and now were keeping most of their ships assembled at the far side of the bay, almost under Gibraltar's heavy guns. Meanwhile they had increased the number of patrolboats and searchlight batteries guarding the ships and had stepped-up the dropping of depth charges.

Added to all this, the night had come down without a breeze, turning the surface of the bay to a glassy flatness, making it almost impossible to approach a target without being detected.

Accordingly, the decision was made to send only three swimmers into the bay, each carrying three fused limpet mines, and to let them attack any targets they could reach.

It was close to midnight when the first member of the group moved quietly across the darkened beach in front of the bungalow and slipped into the water. The other two swimmers followed within minutes. The remaining pair of frogmen stayed hidden in the shadows of the shore, straining for some sign of action to develop near the anchored ships, ready to swim out and help if necessary.

The vigil lasted for almost seven hours before the dim gray light of dawn finally brought the exhausted frogmen back to the shore, and from there up the slope to the shelter of the Villa. One man had spent the entire night dodging patrolboats and trying in vain to slip past them, or under them, and to reach his target ship; finally his oxygen supply had given out, and he had abandoned his mission. Of the other two swimmers, each had attached limpet mines to a ship's hull, but neither could be certain as to which ship he had reached.

As it turned out, both men had attacked the same ship, one forward and one aft. They discovered that fact shortly after daylight when the freighter *Raven's Point* suddenly exploded and started down by the stern, then exploded again and went down by the bow.

"We're getting wasteful," Ramognino said wryly. "One man would have been enough."

Meanwhile during the months of shaping Villa Carmela into an advanced base, the idea for a bigger and much more effective operation had taken form in the mind of Licio Visintini, one of the original Serchio torpedo pilots.

Visintini had been in and out of the Gibraltar area several times since the memorable night, months earlier, when he and Giovanni Magro had sunk the *Denby Dale*. In recent days he had been working closely with Pepo Martini, operating at the Algeciras end of the smuggling route. It was there that he conceived his idea. He promptly sent an urgent message to Borghese and then flew to La Spezia for a special meeting of the two of them alone. They got together one twilight in Borghese's office, sharing a bottle of wine.

"I appreciate your time," said Visintini. "I know you're busy with more important matters."

Borghese shrugged. "Sinking British ships is always important."

"That's what I think too, Commander. And that's what this is all about. I outlined the general idea in my message from Algeciras."

"You did," said Borghese. "Now give me details."

"Fine," said Visintini. "First, let's consider Villa Carmela. It's a good setup and it's paying off. But it has one big drawback: it's only good for the frogman teams. We can't use it for the big stuff, the human-torpedoes."

Borghese nodded in agreement. "True, unfortunately."

"So I propose we set up another Gibraltar base, this time for the torpedo teams." Visintini leaned forward, speaking with excitement. "We'd keep the Carmela operation running, of course. It's successful, and it has the British completely baffled. But think what it would mean to have torpedo teams always available, ready to attack on a moment's call. And we can do it, right in Algeciras! Here's how:

"There's an old Italian freighter, rusting away out there in the bay. She's the Olterra, out of Genoa. She was caught in Gibraltar Roads when Italy went into the war. Her skipper immediately ran her aground in Spanish territorial waters to keep her out of the hands of the British."

"I know about her," Borghese replied. "Ramognino has mentioned her."

"Yes," said Visintini. "He sees her every day. She's half under water now, stranded where she was scuttled, just a short distance from Algeciras Harbor. She still flies the Italian flag and keeps a token crew aboard to protect her owner's property rights. She's been rusting away for months. She's been sitting out there in the bay so long she's part of the scenery. Nobody pays attention to her any more."

Borghese took a drink of wine. "I see where you're heading, Licio. Go on."

"So we negotiate with the owner," said Visintini. "He arranges for a Spanish salvage company to refloat the Olterra and tow her into Algeciras Harbor. He puts out a story about having her repaired and refitted — says he has a good offer from a shipping company that wants to buy her — that there's a lot of work to be done, especially below decks in the engine room and boiler room. Laborers and engineers and deckhands will be coming in from Italy to handle the job."

Borghese nodded with enthusiasm. "And that's where we'll be working, setting up a new advanced base in the hull of the Olterra!"

"Exactly!"

"With men and supplies smuggled in by Pepo Martini and concealed aboard ship?"

"It would work, Commander. I'd stake my life on it."

Borghese reached across the table. "Your hand, Licio. It's a brilliant idea. You are now officially in charge of the project. Get it moving right away. Pick your own crew for the job — anybody you want. And draw whatever you need from the Tenth Light."

Within the next few days, Visintini assembled a crew of skilled River Serchio specialists to handle the Olterra project. He assigned them first to a training schedule aboard an Italian freighter anchored at Leghorn. There they learned to act like calloused merchant seamen. They learned how to dress, how to drink, how to argue, what blasphemies to use, what card games to play, how to cadge a drink from a stranger, how to salvage a cigar butt. By the time they left Leghorn with their forged papers, they could have passed for scruffy, transient mariners at any waterfront saloon in Spain.

Meanwhile the Olterra was hauled free, pumped out and towed into harbor at Algeciras, where she was moored at a pier almost directly under the windows of the British consulate. Then the work of conversion got under way.

By twos and threes, the men of the Olterra's new crew began arriving and making themselves known along the waterfront. They were a ragged, hard-living lot, usually unshaven and usually cramped for money. They seemed to be forever drinking and complaining, cursing the war and all shipowners in general, haggling with the local whores, bawling drunken ballads as they reeled back to ship after a night on the town. To Spanish police and British agents alike, they soon became a familiar part of the dockside scene, as ordinary and harmless as some old derelict slumped against a pier.

But aboard ship it was a different world, a world of hard work and strict military discipline. Out of sight, far below decks and behind concealed doors, Visintini ran a taut operation. And under his direction, astonishing changes took place within the Olterra.

A workshop was constructed to reassemble the human-torpeodoes that would be arriving in sections from Italy. A test tank was constructed in the forward hold. A machine shop took shape, a carpentry shop was established, lathes and generators began to hum, and storage bins were set up for fuel, munitions and spare parts.

Meanwhile, on the port side of the ship, Visintini set aside a cabin for an observation post, with orders that it be manned 24 hours a day. It commanded a clear seaward view of Gibraltar Harbor and the convoy anchorage areas and provided up-to-the-minute information on all British ship movements and harbor defenses. When closer observation seemed called for, one or two of the Serchio seamen would spend the day drifting about the bay in an old fishing dory, sometimes dropping their fishlines directly alongside an anchored convoy ship, sometimes even offering to sell their fish to the crew.

On one occasion, while peering through his binoculars at net-barrier activites near Gibraltar, Visintini idly remarked that he would appreciate a better set of glasses. That night, two of his seamen went ashore and returned with a pair of Navy binoculars of extraordinary magnification — stolen, along with a stabilizing tripod, from the roof of the neighboring British consulate.

Eventually, on a day in late autumn, all was in readiness for the full manning of the *Olterra* base and the start of torpedo operations. Safely stowed aboard were crates and packing cases that had been brought into Spain by Pepo Martini's smugglers — 17 underwater motors of 300 pounds each, 30 explosive warheads of 250 to 750 pounds each, 50 timing mechanisms, 70 underwater lamps, 120 revolvers, 65 rifles, plus assorted fuses, batteries, goggles, fins, oxygen masks and other equipment. Pepo had done a superlative job, right under the noses of British agents and Spanish sentries.

As a final step, Visintini's men went to work with acetylene torches and cut a wide hole in the portside hull of the ship, deep below the waterline. As the sea poured through into a watertight compartment, it opened the way for the human-torpedoes to enter or leave the *Olterra* at will, unseen by anyone from above or ashore.

With preparations for attack all completed, Visintini that night wrote a letter to his wife Maria, back in Italy:

"After four months of uncertainty, struggle and incessant work, my great plan is ripe. Tomorrow evening, three craft and six men will be ready to leave.

"The enemy is an experienced veteran, but we do not fear him. Our hearts are exalted and utterly resolved to conquer at all costs.

"For many evenings now we have been able to calculate, hour by hour and minute by minute, the various forms of peril that await us and are designed to prevent us from reaching our objectives. But bursting bombs and darting patrolboats only strengthen our will to defy the enemy.

"The stakes are enormous. The game is a complicated and subtle one. But nothing can stop us now save death...."

When dark came down, Visintini was the first to pilot a human-torpedo out of the *Olterra* and to set an underwater course across the bay toward Gibraltar's harbor entrance. Behind him rode his diver, Magro. Their target was the British battleship *Nelson*, which had just come through the Straits and was moored at Gibraltar's North Mole.

They arrived at the entrance, to find their way blocked by a deadly curtain of depth charges, bursting at three-minute intervals. Just beyond, tantalizingly close, the *Nelson* rode at anchor, her lights gleaming on the water. Without hesitation, Visintini drove straight ahead at his target. He was killed almost instantly by the depth bombs erupting around him.

The bodies of both men came to the surface a few days later and were recovered by a British naval security patrol. They were buried at sea off Gibraltar with full military ceremonies, and a wreath was tossed to the waves in their honor.

Visintini's *Olterra* project eventually stood as a good memorial to an imaginative hero. It was successful in the sinking of six ships — the British freighters *Mahsud*, *Stanridge* and *Camerata*, the Norwegian tanker *Thorshovdi*, and the American Liberty ships *Pat Harrison* and *Harrison Gray Otis*, a total of nearly 50,000 tons.

But meanwhile, the Americans had landed in North Africa. Convoys of men and supplies were arriving there in incredible numbers. And again the call went out for the Tenth Light Flotilla to bear a hand.

Chapter 21.
Assignment Africa

S carcely had the first American troops landed on the coast of French North Africa in November 1942, than waves of supplies and equipment came rolling ashore to support them.

The waves rose to a torrent and then to a flood. Pouring in on the beaches came everything needed for a long fighting campaign — from food to fuel, munitions to medicine, trucks to tanks. And all came from the swelling fleets of convoy ships that converged on the scene like the surge of a tidal river.

At Algiers, nosing past warships and landing craft, the armed freighters moved in to take up all available dockside space and to begin unloading cargo. Behind the working ships, awaiting their turn, were scores of other vessels that jammed the inner harbor to capacity. The roadstead and the outer harbor spaces were equally thick with tankers, Liberty ships and big freighters, all riding low under the weight of full tonnage and with extra cargo lashed to their decks.

The situation looked ideal for an attack by teams from the Tenth Light. Accordingly, the decision was made at La Spezia to rush the submarine *Ambra* to the scene with 10 frogmen and four human-torpedo crews. To improve the odds for success, attacks were to be made only against merchant ships that were moored in the outer harbor. And since no heavy warships were to be assaulted, the 660-pound warheads on the human-torpedoes were replaced by twin war-heads, each containing 330 pounds of explosive. One of these alone would be ample for sinking a merchantman; in sets of two, they doubled the striking power of each crew. Finally, after releasing the attack-force on the night of December 11-12, the submarine was to wait in the roadstead only until 3 a.m. and then head back for La Spezia.

Thus the *Ambra*, skippered by Lieutenant Commander Mario Aril-lo, put to sea from La Spezia on the evening of December 4, heading southwest for the long trip to the African coast. It was an easy voyage, marred only by violent waves that arose on the night of December 8 and sent several of the frogmen reeling to their bunks, hopelessly seasick. Then the weather calmed and the waves flattened out once more.

Shortly after dawn on the 11th, the sighting of distant convoy ships and the droning of planes overhead told Arillo that he was nearing the invasion beaches. From here on, if he remained on the surface, there would be escort ships, depth charges, gun crews and bomber planes to worry about. He checked his course and plotted a direct approach to Algiers. Then he took the *Ambra* down.

For the next several hours, until late in the afternoon, the subma-rine moved ahead submerged, hugging the floor of the sea, gliding silently ever closer to her objective. As darkness fell, she moved into the outer harbor, slipping beneath the hulls of anchored ships. She had arrived. Arillo signaled "Stop engines" and put her gently on the bottom in 60 feet of water.

Within minutes, reserve pilot Augusto Jacobacci of the human-torpedo group had donned his swim-suit and breathing apparatus and left the *Ambra* through her escape hatch, swimming cautiously up to the surface. He carried a telephone with him, connecting back to Arillo for situation reports.

"Straight ahead at slow speed, Commander." Jacobacci's voice came down from above, sounding low but clear. "We're right on course for a choice of targets."

The *Ambra* moved forward in a gentle glide. Overhead, Jacobacci swam along, keeping pace.

"Come right five degrees," he directed. "It looks interesting over that way."

Arillo shifted to the new course. "Any ships close to you?"

"Yes, sir," came the reply. "But I'm looking for a nest of them. It's very black up here."

"Keep looking."

"Hold it, Commander!" Jacobacci's voice was suddenly urgent. "All stop!"

"All stop...What's wrong?"

"There's a sunken destroyer right in your path. Dead ahead, about 400 yards. I can see her masts and her bridge."

"Very well," said Arillo. "I'll flank her and return to course. Keep us informed."

"Aye, sir. And I can see our targets now, just beyond the destroyer. There's a group of six vessels sitting there. Three of them are real big ones. And others are scattered close about."

"Then that's where we'll go," said Arillo. "Keep alert, now — I'm turning left."

At 2200 hours by the ship's clock, the *Ambra* came to a halt on the bottom directly below the anchored targets and about 2,000 yards from the entrance to the inner harbor. Within an hour, the frogmen one by one had left the submarine through the escape hatch and surfaced beside Jacobacci, who pointed out their target areas. Twenty minutes later, the human-torpedo teams were on their way up, and Jacobacci started back down toward the submarine. As he submerged, he heard machine-gun firing nearby, and felt and heard the jarring explosions of distant depth charges.

Arillo held the *Ambra* on the site until 3 a.m. and then sent Jacobacci to the surface once more for a final look around. No shipmates were to be seen. He returned to the submarine.

"Nothing, Commander," he told Arillo. "Nobody waiting to be picked up."

Arillo nodded. "In that case, we'll go home. It's a long way back."

Meanwhile, the frogmen and torpedo teams had been quietly going about their work of attacking targets.

It was just after midnight when the leader of the swimmers, Lieutenant Agostino Morello, grouped his men around him to assign objectives. They drew close, treading water in the darkness. Nearby were the shadowy shapes of huge vessels, anchored in a rough semi-circle. The sky was overcast, and the water flickered with phosphorescence.

Morello spoke in hushed tones. "All set, now. Ghiglione and Lucia-ni — you two take the ship at the far end of the circle. Rolfini and Evangelisti, you take the one just this side of it, the second in line from the end. Lugano and Lucchetti, the next one is yours, the third in line. Boscole, you go for the fourth — you'll be alone. Botti and Feroldi, you stay with me. The three of us will take the big ship that's anchored just back of the others. I'll attack the port side, Botti the starboard, and Feroldi the stern.

"And all of you — if the submarine is gone when you've finished, just try to get safely ashore and surrender. Move out, now. And good luck."

As the frogmen swam off toward their targets, the torpedo crews rode their vehicles close to that of Lieutenant Giorgio Badessi, their group leader. Each was assigned two ships in the outer harbor, the biggest of which was a U.S. Navy assault transport identified only as N59.

"Reggioli and Pamolli, that one's yours," Badessi said. "And so is the big British tanker just beyond. Arena and Cocchi, you take the two cargo ships sitting side by side over there. Pesel and I will move around until I decide what to attack. Good hunting, and God bless you."

Each crew checked its compass course and quietly submerged. The time was a half-hour after midnight. A light mist drifted in from the sea. The outer harbor was silent, giving no sign that men were busy beneath the surface, attaching fused mines to the hulls of ships.

The first explosion came at 5 a.m. Four others followed in the next two hours, jarring the port with violent shocks, hurling great showers of wreckage into the air. Sirens screamed, rescue boats tore about, and destroyers lashed the area with depth charges. The harbor was thrown into turmoil.

The N59, with her stern blasted away, struggled to the beach and went down in shallow depths with her decks above water. The *Ocean Vanquisher* and the *Berta*, both British, each blew up with a roar and sank from sight. The British freighter *Armattan* and the tanker *Empire Centaur* suffered severe damage to their hulls and were left helpless, each sloping under a heavy list.

In short, five more ships had been put out of action. And 16 more men from River Serchio were rounded up ashore and carried off to prison camps.

It was a solid victory. But back at La Spezia, Borghese was concerned with much more ambitious matters. His plans for attacking New York were now fully under way.

Admiral Angelo Cabrini, Italian delegate to NATO, reminisces about his days as a young frogman. Admiral David Tibbits, Royal Navy, was Navigation Officer aboard the cruiser *York* at Suda Bay. Emilio Bianchi remembers frogman action that won medals for bravery.

Forward battery of *HMS York*, heaviest cruiser guns afloat.

Chapter 22.
Targets of Chromium

In May 1943, Borghese received orders from Rome promoting him to full command of the Tenth Light Flotilla, this time on a permanent basis.

One reason for this move, he realized, was to give him a free hand to use the Tenth Light's skills and facilities in whatever way he might choose for the development of his New York attack project. But meanwhile, there were other areas in which Flotilla personnel could be used to great advantage and which required leadership decisions. In one immediate instance, he recognized a need for speedy action. This was a case dealing with enemy ships that were engaged in transporting chromium.

As Borghese was aware, the light and valuable metal was an essential element for successful war production, both in Britain and in the United States. It was being loaded for shipment to those two countries in the Turkish ports of Alexandretta and Mersina on the Gulf of Alexandretta. There the vessels of various Allied nations were departing regularly with thousands of tons of chromium in their cargo holds. Borghese was confident he could disrupt and cripple the traffic, even though it was emanating from neutral waters. He was equally certain that the assignment could be handled by one man, thus creating virtually no interference at all with demands for the New York project and other Tenth Light programs.

He sent for the man he had in mind for the mission, Lieutenant Luigi Ferraro, Tripolitan athlete and champion swimmer, whose adventurous nature fitted perfectly with the job to be done. They met at Borghese's office in La Spezia, and talked long and quietly in the spring twilight.

"As you can see," Borghese said, summing up, "I cannot send in torpedo teams or E-boats or large numbers of swimmers, because the waters are neutral. If the Turks caught us intruding, there would be a terrible diplomatic uproar. We must avoid that.

"But if one lone frogman can get in there with limpet mines and destroy two or three ships, it will rob the enemy of thousands of tons of critical metal. Also — and very important — if the war is brought right to the Turkish harbors, it will tend to discourage them from making further shipments to our enemies. I'm convinced that one man can do it, if he has the nerve and skill."

Ferraro smiled. "And you've decided I'm that man, Commander? You flatter me."

"No." Borghese shook his head. "It's not flattery, it's sound judgement. You are the best swimmer we have in the Navy. You are a trained saboteur. You have the courage, the daring. And you are just enough self-assured and prone to excitement to enjoy the challenge. You're the right man for this mission — nobody else."

"It does hold a certain fascination," Ferraro agreed. "And it appeals to the ego. But how do you propose to get me there? Do I just walk up and say, 'Good morning, gentlemen. I'd like to blow up your ship'?"

"I've got it all figured out," said Borghese. "We will obtain papers from Rome attaching you to the staff of the Italian Vice-Consul at Alexandretta, the Marquis Ignazio di Sanfelice.

"The papers, of course, will be forged. There are two reasons for this. First, because we don't want any government official in Rome to know what's going on; there are too many defeatists who are thinking of selling out to the enemy and who would get in our way. Secondly, because your papers must represent official documents from the Ministry of Foreign Affairs — and the Ministry, you can be sure, would never agree to the subterfuge."

"So apparently you have found a way to get the papers." Ferraro accepted a glass of wine.

"We have," said Borghese. "It was simple. One of our petty officers here in the Tenth Light is having a very warm affair with a beautiful secretary who works at the Ministry. Without knowing what we're up to, she has agreed to help us. She's providing us with the forged credentials and all necessary papers — also with the Ministry stamp to make everything look official."

Ferraro chuckled. "I'm intrigued by the intrigue."

"I thought you would be," said Borghese. "You will leave for Alexandretta in three days and report to the consulate for special duties on behalf of the Ministry.' Your contact at the consulate is a clerk named Giovanni Roccardi. He's actually a lieutenant in Naval Intelligence, and to a large extent this whole plan is his idea. He's the only man who knows you're coming — or why."

Ferraro raised his eyebrows. "Not even the Marquis? He doesn't know?"

"Nobody but Roccardi. He'll give you all the details when you meet him."

"I like it," Ferraro said. "I've always wanted to be a Hollywood actor. This will be even better."

Thus on a day in early June, Ferraro arrived at the Alexandretta consulate accompanied by four heavy suitcases, each protected by diplomatic seal. He presented his credentials to a bewildered Marquis di Sanfelice who found all papers in order but couldn't understand why he hadn't been notified in advance that Ferraro was coming. He was also puzzled by the Ministry's request to "give all possible assistance" to Ferraro, especially since it soon appeared that the newcomer had nothing to do but lie on the beach and soak up the sun — usually with Giovanni Roccardi for company.

Within a few days after arrival, Ferraro had been introduced by Roccardi to the leaders of Alexandretta's consular set and social circles. The new man from Italy quickly became very popular, in constant demand at the beach and at cocktail parties and dances. He was charming to the ladies, and well liked by most of the men. He was a companionable drinker and a considerate gentleman. He blended into diplomatic life as though born for the role.

It pleased his new friends that he was on the beach almost every day, in the morning for the sun and in the evening for handball or bowls. Generally at sundown, he would come out of the Italian consulate's bathhouse carrying a big box of beach balls, nets and gear, unload it on the sands, and get started with games that would last until dusk, when he would re-pack the box and walk back to the bathhouse in the gathering darkness. He seldom ventured into the water, and apparently was just a wader — certainly not a good swimmer. Everybody grew used to his habits — just as they were used to the six consulate residences that rimmed the waterfront — and just as they were used to the ships that moored out in the middle of the harbor, loading chromium from barges and lighters.

Soon, back at La Spezia, Borghese received a coded report from Roccardi:

"Ferraro's arrival has certainly made the operation possible from a technical point of view. From the organizational point of view we have succeeded in introducing into our small diplomatic world — which is extremely prone to gossip — a new subject of curiosity, and have done so without excessive shock. Ferraro is now a part of the scenery.

"The atmosphere in which we are working is that of a small frontier city, enlivened by the intrigues of six consulates — American, British, French, Greek, German and Italian, all of which sit cozily side by side along the beach front. The population of 12,000, mostly Arabs, is not hostile. It is even potentially friendly. But it is kept in subjection by the suspicious attitude of the Turkish police and influenced by enemy propaganda, disseminated by Greeks and Jews who are very bitter against us and who, for the most part, are voluntary spies for the British. The latter have all the top local authorities practically in their pockets.

"However, I have managed to get everything arranged satisfactorily, and our work is going on right under the noses of two agents of British Secret Intelligence — who are neither secret nor intelligent — and whose special duty it is to watch Italian citizens in general, and presumably our two selves in particular, despite our innocent behavior.

"My task is much facilitated by Ferraro's genial and expansive character, which is certainly the last that might be expected to be meditating dark projects involving dynamite."

Borghese filed the report with satisfaction, and turned again to his New York plans. He knew he would no longer have to be concerned with chromium.

On the afternoon of June 30, the Greek freighter *Orion* lay at anchor in the Alexandretta harbor, some 2,000 yards from shore and on a line northwest from the beach in front of the Italian Consulate. She was a 7,000-ton vessel, newly arrived that day to take on her cargo of metal. Already her holds and winches were being made ready for work, and lighters in the dockside section of the port were preparing to take their loads alongside.

That twilight, Ferraro and Roccardi were having one of their customary games of beach ball, but this time the competition seemed sharper than usual, so much so that the pair were still at it well past their normal quitting time. The spectators who had been watching and applauding them finally began to lose interest and to drift away, one after another, to get ready for the evening routine of cocktails and dinner.

As darkness finally fell, the game came to a halt and Roccardi sauntered away from the beach. Ferraro as usual packed up his game box and carried it to the consulate bathhouse. He disappeared inside. Minutes later he came out again, this time clad in a skin-tight suit of black rubber. There were fins on his feet and a breathing mask on his face. There were clumps of seaweed on his head and two limpet mines hanging from his belt. He took a careful look around; the beach was deserted. He walked quickly to the water's edge and entered, swimming off quietly into the blackness of the harbor.

It was a long journey to the *Orion*'s anchorage but Ferraro took his time, going slowly with caution, adjusting his course to avoid the shifting beams of searchlights, treading water occasionally, and finally sliding along the side of the ship's hull so close to the enemy that he could hear the voices of seamen on deck. Then he dove down in the blackness and clamped his explosives in place, one on either side of the keel. He activated their propeller mechanisms to produce explosions as soon as the ship's rate of speed reached five knots. Then he turned back for the long swim to shore. At 4 a.m., he was in the consulate kitchen, sharing a drink with Roccardi.

It took the *Orion* a full week to finish loading and to prepare for departure. But she never reached the open sea. She was just clearing the outer harbor when she blew up with a thundering roar and sank in a whirlpool of wreckage and chromium waste. News of the sinking reached Borghese that night via short-wave radio.

Within hours after the *Orion* had gone down, Roccardi received a message from one of his agents at Mersina, on the western shore of the gulf, reporting the arrival there of the British freighter *Kaituna*. She was a big, new, up-to-date ship of 10,000 tons, equipped with strong defensive gun batteries and rigged with the most modern gear for cargo handling. She was taking on a full load of chromium.

Thus, early the next morning, July 9, Ferraro and Roccardi informed the Marquis di Sanfelice that they had important Ministry business to conduct elsewhere, and that they would be away from the consulate for one night, perhaps two.

The Marquis thought it strange that they took only one sealed suitcase with them; but since he had strict orders to cooperate, he shrugged and asked no questions.

Late that afternoon, the two men were on the beach at Mersina, enjoying a leisurely swim. At sundown, they were resting on the sand, watching the twilight shadows move in across the water. Dusk fell, sending other bathers on their way for the evening and gradually dimming the outline of the big ship that was moored far out in the harbor, busily loading cargo. It was full dark when Ferraro finally appeared alone on the empty beach, adjusted his fins and mask, and slipped into the water. He disappeared within seconds, swimming straight out and leaving scarcely a ripple behind him.

Less than 18 hours later, he and Roccardi were back on the beach at Alexandretta, tossing a handball back and forth and joking with friends who had not even missed them.

As it happened, the *Kaituna* took 10 days to load her cargo. She weighed anchor on the 19th and moved slowly out of harbor, swinging down past Cape Karatas to the open sea. She was just off the northern coast of Cyprus and rapidly picking up speed when the mines on her hull exploded. She managed to avoid sinking by running aground on the Cyprus shore, a staggered wreck. But the score had been made; she was permanently out of the war, and her cargo lay stranded in debris.

By August 2, Ferraro had only two limpet mines left in his sealed luggage, sufficient for one more attack. And on that day, the Norwegian motorship *Fernplant* moved into harbor at Alexandretta and dropped anchor for taking on cargo. She was a 7,000-ton ship, moored in almost the same position the *Orion* had occupied earlier, but slightly closer to the consulate beach.

Ferraro and Roccardi, lazing on the sands, eyed her with appreciation. She was an excellent target. Tons of chromium already were being ferried out for loading aboard. The weather forecast called for a black night and a calm sea. They voiced agreement that it was time for one more drawn-out game of beachball that would run on until deep twilight; and time for Ferraro to take his final swim.

The *Fernplant*, fully loaded, cleared the harbor at 6 o'clock on the evening of August 5, heading for the open sea. Ferraro and Roccardi stood at a window of the consulate, watching her out of sight. A short time later, the stillness of night was shattered by the boom of a tremendous explosion, somewhere out in the gulf. Nobody ever saw the *Fernplant* again.

Back at the consulate, Roccardi mixed two drinks and carried them out to the porch, to sit with Ferraro and talk.

"Well done, Luigi," he said. "What now?"

Ferraro sipped his drink in the darkness and stared out across the harbor. "I think now it would be a good time for me to catch malaria," he said. "Of course, if I'm very sick I'll have to be sent to Italy. You'd explain that to our friends."

Roccardi nodded agreement. "But we mustn't be too abrupt," he said. "Suppose you get sick about three days from now. Does that sound like a good schedule?"

"Fine with me," said Ferraro. "It will give me a couple of days to relax. Maybe take some swimming lessons."

That night, back at La Spezia, Borghese received the news of the *Fernplant* sinking and reviewed the earlier reports on the *Orion* and the *Kaituna*. He decided that Ferraro would be an excellent man to take along on the voyage to New York.

British cruiser *HMS York*, heavy-gunned target of Suda Bay attack.

Chapter 23.
Attack That Never Came

In the months preceding Ferraro's triple victory over the chromium ships, Italy's Atlantic Submarine Base at Bordeaux had become one of the biggest Axis strongholds on the coast of France.

Here, miles inland from the Bay of Biscay on the shore of the River Gironde, were quartered the best commanders and crewmen in the ocean-going branch of the undersea fleet. Some of them fought along-side Admiral Doenitz' U-boats in wolfpack attacks against Allied convoys in the North Atlantic. Some of them operated lone patrols reaching to the South Atlantic and the Indian Ocean. Still others were engaged in long-distance cargo hauls, traveling as far away as Japan to deliver sophisticated German war instruments and returning with cargoes of rubber, sulphur, pure whale oil and other natural products to help the Axis war production. Between assignments, these men relaxed on the comfortable estates that nestled in the wooded Bordeaux countryside.

It was here that Borghese now spent much of his time preparing for the attack on New York, and for a projected follow-up operation against Britain's huge South Atlantic Squadron Base at Freetown in Sierra Leone.

Months earlier, he had been assigned the big, long-range submarine *Da Vinci* to incorporate into his New York program. His immediate problem was to fit out the *Da Vinci*'s interior for carrying frogmen and other saboteurs and to reshape her deck to enable her to take aboard a 12-ton CA2 midget assault submarine, armed with two torpedoes. The *Da Vinci* then would be equipped to transport the assault-teams to the mouth of New York Harbor, release them, and perhaps rendezvous with the CA2 after the attack.

It was still mid-winter when the work of reshaping the *Da Vinci* was completed and she was pronounced ready for sea trials. The submarine's regular skipper, Commander Gianfranco Gazzana-Priaroggia, was ordered temporarily relieved from duty, and Borghese assumed command. One cold, clear dawn, he took the big submarine down the river and out to sea, noting that she must look like a strange vessel indeed, gliding along with a bed scooped out of her deck and with a midget submarine clamped into the hollow.

"Like a baby kangaroo in its mother's pouch," he remarked. "The question is, can it hop out and get back in."

It could, and it did. After several hours of surfacing and submerging, in the grey waters between Bordeaux and La Palice, Borghese took the *Da Vinci* down to an assumed departure depth and gave the order to launch. The CA2 immediately broke free of its clamps and rose directly to the surface, shedding water like a contented seal. The *Da Vinci* moved up alongside and put aboard the midget submarine's crew. Within minutes, the CA2 was in full operation, now submerging, now surfacing, now sailing rapid circles around the big mothership.

Again Borghese took the *Da Vinci* down, trying this time to position her directly beneath the midget.

"Surface for recovery!" he ordered.

The *Da Vinci* rose slowly, coming up directly in line with the CA2 and catching the small vessel smoothly in the hollow of the deck. Clamps were snapped into place and the *Da Vinci* went down again and headed back toward Bordeaux, carrying the "baby" securely on her back. Succeeding tests during the next several days and nights were equally successful, with never a hitch in the maneuver.

Fully satisfied, Borghese sent off a report to Rome: "The operation against New York has passed out of the planning stage into that of practical preparation."

At that point, he returned the command of the *Da Vinci* to Gazzana-Priaroggia and departed from Bordeaux. He estimated that it would be at least three months before he would be needed again at the big submarine base. Meanwhile there were other demands to be answered and much traveling to do. He would have to go to San Sebastian in Spain for a meeting with Pepo Martini and a checkup on the Algeciras smuggling activities. He would need to visit Madrid and talk with the Italian naval attache Captain Aristide Bona, who had gathered valuable information about New York's harbor defenses. He would have to call on the naval attache in Lisbon, Captain Cugia di Sant'Orsola, for information about enemy ship traffic in that port. He was expected in Berlin, to review a progress report on the training of German assault-teams. And in Paris, for another meeting with Admiral Doenitz. And back in La Spezia, for the routine business of the Tenth Light and the evaluating of operators for New York.

On February 20, as Borghese was leaving Bordeaux by rail, Gazzana-Priaroggia was leaving the base by submarine, checking navigational bearings from the *Da Vinci*'s bridge as he took his ship down the Gironde and out to sea. His orders were to travel alone and to search for enemy convoys in the South Atlantic, or move on to the Indian Ocean, wherever the hunting proved good. He was scheduled to return to Bordeaux at the end of May for another meeting with Borghese.

For the next three months, the *Da Vinci* remained out of touch, occupied with its war patrol. Then on May 22, the submarine's radio operator raised the communications station at Bordeaux from a position between the Canary Islands and the Azores, moving northeast toward home. The message was from Gazzana-Priaroggia, brief but clear:

"Will arrive Bordeaux on 29 May. Acknowledge."

That was the last word ever received from the *Da Vinci*. Homeward bound, she sailed headlong into the outer range of the biggest convoy battle ever to rage in the North Atlantic, a titanic five-day fight that began south of Greenland and carried the embattled ships and submarines all the way down to the Azores area before coming to an end in a convoy victory. In the course of that struggle, the British destroyers *Active* and *Ness* attacked and sank an unidentified submarine on May 23 at a point 300 miles northwest of Cape Finisterre, exactly where the *Da Vinci* would have been.

News of the *Da Vinci*'s loss reached Borghese a few nights later as he was dining at the Officers Club in Berlin. It was a setback to his plans for New York, but by no means a serious one. Another submarine would be provided and restructured, and another crew would be trained. He was satisfied that the program would continue and would soon be back on schedule. Still, the sinking of the *Da Vinci* left him with an uneasy feeling, as though it were a portent of more trouble to come. And somehow it seemed incongruous, to be hearing a tragic report of modern sea warfare within the rich, oppressive atmosphere of a club where portraits of long-dead German generals and emperors stared down from massive walls.

Borghese handed the *Da Vinci* report to his dinner companion, an Austrian colonel. Then he gestured wryly at the pretentious framed pictures and the outdated surroundings. "Another submarine missing. How many times do you suppose a report like that has been received in this room? And with what indifference? It's almost as though nothing has changed in here since 1918. Germany did not understand naval warfare then, and she does not understand it now."

The Austrian nodded in agreement. "You are more right than you imagine," he said. "Germany only understands ground warfare. And because of that, there now seems to be a hint of defeatism in the air, a faint but worrisome sense of uncertainty.

"Let's admit it, the war is not going well. We had hoped for a lightning victory over Russia, but it did not come. We had hoped for a British surrender; it did not come. We had hoped that America would stay out of the battle; but America is in. We had hoped for brilliant strategic leadership; but instead we get the aberrations of a schizophrenic corporal. We seem to be piling up troubles. Do they think that way in Rome?"

"Some of them do," Borghese acknowledged. "Some of them would like to quit now and be friends again with the United States. Worse yet, some would like to change sides and fight against the Germans. I cannot understand that. We made our choice. As a matter of honor, we must stand with Germany as long as the war goes on. How long do you suppose that will be?"

The Austrian frowned. "Who can say? We shall go on fighting to the end, of course, for that is our duty and we can do nothing else.

"But the game was lost as soon as it began. In spite of the terrible experience of the First World War, the Germans have repeated the same fundamental errors of those years. Germany considers the function of military strategy to be confined to land operations, forgetting that Britain cannot be defeated except by sea.

"The restricted mentality which conceives modern warfare in terms of armies fighting to conquer border territories must inevitably succumb to that which studies the great problems of a three-dimensional strategy — by air, by sea and on land — and takes the entire globe for its province.

"Perhaps, after we have paid a terrible price for this error, which will leave disastrous traces in Germany — perhaps after that, we shall be able to show in the Third World War that we have finally learned the lessons that history has been trying to teach us.

"But enough of my philosophy. These *Da Vinci* men — they were friends of yours?"

"Good friends and good seamen," Borghese replied. "We were making great plans together."

"There will be other good friends and good seamen," the Austrian said. "You will go on and so shall I."

"Yes," said Borghese. "The uncertainty is not with us but with our leaders. Which way will they take us?"

Before the summer was over, Borghese learned the answer to his question. Back at La Spezia that July, even while he was enjoying the reports from Roccardi and Ferraro at Alexandretta, he could sense around him the air of defeatism and uncertainty that his Austrian companion had referred to in Berlin. The war was going badly. The leaders were uneasy, wondering nervously about retribution, nursing doubts about what would happen to them.

Against this shifting background, Borghese took time away from his desk for a brief pilgrimage back to River Serchio, to walk alone in the pine forest at sundown, and to sit by the clear running water and reflect on what might lie ahead.

In terms of men and equipment, he assured himself, the Tenth Light was stronger at this moment than it had ever been. That he knew. Improved human-torpedoes and new submarines had arrived at La Spezia and were ready for service. A big new Flotilla base had just been created at Venice. Frogmen and sabotage specialists at that very moment were en route from Venice to neutral ports to attack enemy shipping, and were infiltrating enemy-held ports as well. Flotilla morale was high, untouched by the mood of defeat that was spreading through Rome. The *Da Vinci* had been replaced by a larger and swifter submarine, and the New York project was gaining strength and momentum with every day.

Yes, he told himself — the Tenth Light Flotilla had never been as combat-ready as it was at this moment. Gibraltar was still under attack from the *Olterra*. And teams of Serchio specialists known as the "Giobbe Column" were harassing enemy ships off the coast of North Africa. So much for the good part.

On the other hand, he reminded himself, there were shades to the picture that were as dark and deep and undeniable as the shadows under the heavy Serchio pine trees. A man would be a fool to pretend otherwise.

Looking back, there had been that glorious moment of opportunity created by the Tenth Light almost 20 months ago, when the attack on Alexandria had stripped Britain of her Mediterranean battleships — had left the entire sea ready for Axis domination. But Germany had never understood naval warfare; and so, nobody had moved to grasp the victory.

Since then, it had all been downhill. The United States had entered the war, reviving the Allied lines with new strength. The following October, Rommel had retreated with his battered columns all the way from Alamein to Tunis. Then the Allies had invaded North Africa, storming in at Casablanca and Bone and Algiers. At Stalingrad, the Russians had risen from defeat to crush the German advance and turn it back. Now, the Americans were winning the critical Battle of the Atlantic. And just this month, Allied forces had swept through Sicily and already were landing troops on mainland Italy.

In balance, he told himself, the Axis undoubtedly would lose the war. Perhaps, as the Austrian colonel had said, the game was lost when it began. There was nothing to do now but to admit it, and to hope that he still might lead an attack on New York before the battles ended.

He sat on, for a long time, that night at River Serchio. He remembered with pleasure what it had been like in the early days there, with men like Toschi and Tesei, like de la Penne, Visintini, Martellotta, Bianchi and all the others — their songs and wry humor, their dedication and daring. He remembered with pride all the troubles they had overcome and the victories they had won. Finally he stirred himself from his thoughts, stood up in the darkness and brushed the pine needles from his uniform. It was time to halt the nostalgia, time to leave Serchio and get back to La Spezia to get on with the war, whichever way it might go.

That way quickly became clear. There was a message waiting for him when he returned to La Spezia that night. It directed his attention to a royal statement from Rome, issued that very day by King Victor Emmanuel:

"25 July — His Majesty the King has accepted the resignation of His Excellency Benito Mussolini of his duties as Head of Government, Prime Minister and Secretary of State, and has appointed as Head of Government, Prime Minister and Secretary of State, His Excellency the Marshal of Italy, Pietro Badoglio... At this solemn crisis in the affairs of Italy everyone must stand firm at his post of duty, faith and battle."

And from Badoglio came the message:

"The war goes on. Italy, reeling under the blows inflicted upon her invaded provinces and destroyed cities, remains faithful to her pledged word and jealously preserves her thousand-year-old tradition."

Borghese read the statements with a cynical smile. They sounded to him like the words of politicians, not of fighting men. They were obviously designed to open the way for truce talks with the Allies. And apparently, with Mussolini out of the way, negotiations for an Armistice would soon begin. So be it.

He gave a shrug of mild disdain, then turned and locked the door to his room. He pulled down the window shades and took a bottle of chilled white wine from his refrigerator. Then he sat alone at his desk, trying to imagine the lights of New York Harbor.

A few weeks later, on the 8th of September, Borghese finished a long day of work at his La Spezia headquarters and leaned back to relax in his office chair. He had just completed all the necessary assignments, orders and paper work for a massive torpedo attack on Gibraltar. It was scheduled to take place on October 2 — a surprise daylight attack that would decoy the British defensive units to the outer harbor, leaving the warships unprotected against the main assault. It was a daring idea, and it had been hard work putting the plans into shape. But now it was ready; and the advance teams would leave for the *Olterra* in the morning.

"Once more into the lion's mouth," he murmured to himself. "It's just crazy enough to succeed."

Idly, for something to do, he switched on his radio.

The news came blasting out like a hammer, smashing at his brain, jarring him to his feet in a cold shock. Italy had signed the Armistice! Truce terms were already in force. Allied troops were advancing north, cheered by Italians along the way —

"Nobody told me...!" He stammered. "How strange! Nobody..."

An aide stared at him from across the room. "Sir? Commander? Are you all right?"

Borghese turned to look at him blankly. Then he recovered himself. "Yes...Yes, I'm all right. It's nothing. Tell you what, though — you go to my quarters and pack my bags. And get me a staff car right away. I'll drive it myself — and I'll be gone a long time."

"Aye, sir. And where will you be going?"

"To join the Germans," Borghese said. "To join the Germans. New York will have to wait."

"New York, sir?"

"It was just an idea."

Appendix

SHIPS SUNK OR OTHERWISE PUT OUT OF ACTION BY
TENTH LIGHT FLOTILLA (All British except as noted)

AT SUDA BAY, MARCH 1941
  Cruiser York
  Tanker Pericles
  Tanker — name missing
  Steamship — name missing
AT GIBRALTAR, SEPTEMBER 1941
  Tanker Denby Dale
  Tanker Fiona Shell
  Motorship Durham
AT ALEXANDRIA, DECEMBER 1941
  Battleship Queen Elizabeth
  Battleship Valiant
  Tanker Sagona
  Destroyer Jervis
AT SEBASTOPOL, JUNE 1942

Military Transport — name missing (Russian)
Smallcraft — names missing (Russian)
Two submarines — names missing (Russian)
AT GIBRALTAR, JULY 1942
Steamship Meta
Steamship Empire Snipe
Steamship Shuma
Steamship Baron Douglas
AT EL DABA, AUGUST 1942
Destroyer Eridge
AT GIBRALTAR, SEPTEMBER 1942
Steamship Raven's Point
AT ALGIERS, DECEMBER 1942
Steamship Ocean Vanquisher
Steamship Berta
Steamship Armattan
Tanker Empire Centaur
Military Transport N. 59 — (U.S.)
AT GIBRALTAR, MAY 1943
Steamship Pat Harrison — (U.S.)
Steamship Mahsud
Steamship Camerata
AT ALEXANDRETTA, JULY 1943
Motorship Orion — (Greek)
AT MERSINA, JULY 1943
Motorship Kaituna
AT ALEXANDRETTA, AUGUST 1943
Motorship Fernplant — (Norwegian)
AT GIBRALTAR, AUGUST 1943
Steamship Harrison Gray Otis — (U.S.)
Steamship Stanridge
Tanker Thorshovdi — (Norwegian)

EXCERPTS FROM TAPED INTERVIEWS CONDUCTED BY P. J. CARISELLA:

Commander Marc Antonio Bragadin, Rome, April 1975 —
"I was in command of the 14th Flotilla in the occupation of Crete, with the Germans. So I was the first Italian naval officer to see the destruction of the York. I even have the flag from the ship. When the Germans occupied Crete, they said their bombers had sunk the York.

But I was the only officer able to go aboard the York because there were no other boats left in Suda Bay — the English had sunk all their ships, everything in the harbor.

"Aboard the York, in a desk drawer, I found a message from the Commanding Officer to his Executive Officer dated March 28 and saying 'Please take the statements from all the men who were in the boiler rooms and the engine rooms when the ship was struck on the 26th. I would like you also to make rough notes now, while events are fresh in your mind, of sequence of damage reports. Also, a log of events since we started pumping out.' That was interesting, this message giving credit to the Italians. Written by hand, incidentally...

"Borghese and I were at the Naval Academy together. I knew him since I was 15 years old. As a commander, he was absolutely outstanding. And what he did in command of a submarine — he went three times inside Gibraltar Bay — he went under the mines at Alexandria — this is something absolutely exceptional. I believe no other man in the world, regardless of nation, could have done what he did...

"At the time of the Armistice, he felt he had to continue the war, go with the Germans. But he did very little against the Allies. He was captured and put in prison for a few months. But he was such a hero that the Italian Navy did not press charges against him. He fled to Spain just before he died. He was good looking, courageous. Like a Renaissance Prince. His men would have gone to hell with him. Even after the war, if he'd raised his hand and said 'Follow me!' they would have gone with him...

"Yes, I knew about the New York attack. It was very well organized. If the war had lasted a little longer, the men from the Tenth would have gone in there. It would have been rather easy."

Luigi Durand de la Penne, Rome, April 1975 —

"On the way to Alexandria we talked about many things. We knew it was to be a dangerous mission because this was the third attempt for a submarine to go into Alexandria. But, we felt, the third time never fails. Two subs before us sunk. But it was a necessary operation. We had the same problems as the others...

"When we were above water at night, we would walk and smoke and talk. We knew we were not going to win the war. The times were good for us, but we knew in the long run we would lose. In one or two years, it would be all over for us. At this time, 1941, Germany was winning. But we knew it was not enough. Borghese and I talked about this, but we tried to do the best we could — a sense of duty. But we knew it was impossible to win the war."

Mario Marino at the Navy Club, Salerno, April 1975 —

"When the war started, I asked for duty with the assault group and was assigned to La Spezia. My training for the Alexandria mission was at River Serchio. We had no problems at Alexandria — only the depth charges. We were calm throughout the mission. We were confident of the outcome.

"I was the one that put the explosive below the tanker Sagona. While I was doing this, the destroyer Jervis pulled alongside to refuel.

"The first explosion was the Valiant. I was being held by Egyptian police at the time. Then the Queen Elizabeth exploded. The Sagona was the last to explode. I heard it from the guardhouse."

Emilio Bianchi, Rome, April 1975 —

"In 1936, I asked for and was accepted as a member of the assault group. The work was all very secret. My wife, parents and friends did not know the work I was engaged in.

"On the way to Alexandria in the submarine Scire we talked very little. Commander Borghese would visit our compartment occasionally and talk about the operation. We had no fear. We had trained for this operation for many months. I have always felt that I was never any more skilled or braver than the men who were left behind."

Antonio Marceglia, Venice, April 1975 —

"We had hoped to find the aircraft carrier Eagle in the harbor at Alexandria. But on the night of 18 December, the Eagle left and went through the Suez Canal for the Far East...

"Borghese was very, very clever as a submarine commander. Very serious. Studied all the details. And he made sure that his men received the best food possible.

"I did not know until after the war that Borghese planned to attack New York Harbor. I was a prisoner of war at the time this planning was going on."

Admiral Luigi Faggioni, Chiavari, April 1974 —

"When the war broke out, I was an aide to the Duke of Ancona in Abyssinia. I asked to be sent back to Italy and join the assault group at La Spezia...

"It was hoped that a good part of the British Fleet would be at anchor in Suda Bay and that sufficient damage could be inflicted to give our merchant ships a good chance of getting through. Although we didn't accomplish too much to the fleet, our attack did prove that fast, small torpedo motorboats could carry out attacks in enemy harbors and be successful."

Admiral Angelo Cabrini, Taranto, April 1975 —
"We all volunteered for the Flotilla duty. At the beginning of the war, there were six or seven officers. Later the whole group was enlarged to about 200 men covering all assault programs. It was a small group.

"At Suda Bay, Faggioni explained the targets to us. He knew where all the ships were and he said, 'Cabrini and Tedeschi, go in this direction and attack the York.' We weren't able to see well, so we approached slowly. Once we saw the York clearly, we opened the throttle for full speed. Both of our boats were aimed at the York. Perhaps both hit at the same time. I saw both boats only a few yards from one another and going in the direction of the York. I saw them with my own eyes. I was in the water at the time, and my last look was seeing both assault boats on target."

Lieutenant Commander Robin Buckley, London, April 1974 —
"The York was in Suda Bay to refuel and take on supplies. We knew nothing about the smaller Italian assault boats. They were new to us. They came into the harbor quietly and unseen. Due to the darkness and the mountains in the background, it was almost impossible to see them. And the York had those terribly loud boiler room fans that made it impossible to hear them... I was on the bridge on the port side and looking out ahead. At the speed those crafts came in, nobody saw the attack."

Elios Toschi, Rome, April 1975 —
"Tesei was my best friend. He killed himself in the Malta operation. I often quarreled with him about this, and told him it was not necessary to kill one's self in order to achieve success. But he was willing to sacrifice himself. It's difficult to explain that. One has to remember the times. In those times, men would sacrifice their lives for the success of a mission. Malta was an impossible operation. Tesei told me it was for that reason that it must be tried. That was the last time I saw him."

Prince Valerio Borghese, commander of submarine *Scire*. E-boat raiders in Suda Bay attack. (1) Luigi Faggioni; (2) Angelo Cabrini; (3) Alessio DeVito; (4) Tullio Tedeschi; (5) Lino Beccati; (6) Emilio Barberi.

References

The Italian Navy in World War II by Marc' Antonio Bragadin (U.S. Naval Institute)

From the Ashes of Disgrace by Admiral Franco Maugeri (Reynal & Hitchcock)

A Sailor's Odyssey by Admiral Andrew Browne Cunningham, RN (Dutton)

Sea Devils by J. Valerio Borghese, translated by James Cleugh (Henry Regnery)

Ninth Time Lucky by Elios Toschi (William Kimber, London)

East of Malta, West of Suez by "Bartimeus" (Little, Brown)

History of U. S. Naval Operations in World War II, Volume IX, by Samuel Eliot Morison (Little, Brown)

Epics of Salvage by David Masters (Little, Brown)

Chronology of the War at Sea, 1939-1945 by J. Ronwer and G. Hummelchen (Arco)

I Mezzi D'Assalto (Ufficio Storico Marina Militare)

Imperial War Museum, London

Historical Branch, British Admiralty, London

Ministry of Defense, London

Ministry of Marine Defense, Rome

U. S. Embassy, Rome

Official reports of Tenth Light Flotilla attack-teams upon completion of missions

Letters from:
Commander W. G. Hewson, RN
Commander Roger Harrison, RN
Spartaco Schergart, Tenth Light Flotilla
Tullio Tedeschi, Tenth Light Flotilla
Alessio DeVito, Tenth Light Flotilla
Lino Beccati, Tenth Light Flotilla

Taped interviews:
Captain Reginald Portal, RN
Captain David Tibbits, RN
Commander Robin Buckley, RN
Admiral Luigi Faggioni, Tenth Light Flotilla
Admiral Angelo Cabrini, Tenth Light Flotilla
Elios Toschi, Tenth Light Flotilla
Antonio Marceglia, Tenth Light Flotilla
Emilio Bianchi, Tenth Light Flotilla
Luigi Durand de la Penne, Tenth Light Flotilla
Mario Marino, Tenth Light Flotilla
Vincenzo Martellotta, Tenth Light Flotilla

Previous books by William G. Schofield:
Ashes in the Wilderness
The Cat in the Convoy
Payoff in Black
The Deer Cry
Seek for a Hero
Sidewalk Statesman
Destroyers — Sixty Years
Eastward the Convoys
Treason Trail
Freedom by the Bay

Previous books by P. J. Carisella (With James W. Ryan):
Who Killed the Red Baron?
The Black Swallow of Death

Index

Wartime aerial view of British anchorage at Malta.

P. J. Carisella (left) interviews former frogman and POW
Elios Toschi at meeting in Rome.

Rear row, from left, Teseo Tesei, Elios Toschi, Duke of Spoleto,
Alberto Franzini, Gino Birindelli; front, from left, Alcide Pedretti,
Ario Lazzari, Giovanni Lazzaroni Damos Paccagnini.

At reunion of Suda Bay attack teams, decades after the event: from left, Emilio Barberi, Lino Beccati, Alessio DeVito, Angelo Cabrini, Luigi Faggioni, Tullio Tedeschi.

Luigi Durand de la Penne, from frogman to Italian statesman.

Mario Marino, in Rome, recalls old days as a frogman with the Tenth Light.

Rifts are healed at social meeting in Rome as England's Princess Margaret Rose, standing with Ethiopia's Emperor Haile Selassie, greets Italian Admiral Angelo Cabrini, a former frogman who helped to sink *HMS York*.